The Emerging
Middle East
Financial Markets

HENRY T. AZZAM

authorHOUSE®

AuthorHouse™
1663 Liberty Drive
Bloomington, IN 47403
www.authorhouse.com
Phone: 1 (800) 839-8640

Published by AuthorHouse 08/26/2015

ISBN: 978-1-5049-3281-3 (sc)
ISBN: 978-1-5049-3280-6 (hc)
ISBN: 978-1-5049-3282-0 (e)

Library of Congress Control Number: 2015913664

ACKNOWLEDGMENTS

I want to acknowledge the continuous encouragement and support of my wife Reem who spent time and effort typing, reviewing and offering helpful feedback on the manuscript. She never ceases to astonish me with her resourcefulness and inquisitive mind. She is sincere and passionate in everything she does and her love to life is contagious. I remain endlessly grateful for her being the spirit in me behind all that is moral, humane and joyful.

This book is dedicated to my sons Suhail, Ramzi and Marwan who have embarked on their own journey to help change the world, and to little Sofia, our adorable grand daughter and my reason for wanting to believe in angels.

I am hopeful that students of Middle East Finance, asset managers, businessmen, bankers, politicians and government officials will find this book a useful reference when studying the structure and investment opportunities of the region's emerging financial markets .

To those investors seeking to have exposure to the financial markets of the MENA region and are looking for diversification and attractive risk adjusted returns, this book promises to give them an edge to outperform.

Other Books written by the Author

1. The Gulf Economies in Transition, The Macmillan Press (London, 1988).

2. Saudi Arabia: Economic Trends, Business Environment and Investment opportunities, Euromoney (London, 1993).

3. The Emerging Arab Capital Markets, Kegan Paul International (New York, 1997).

4. The Arab World Facing The Challenge Of The New Millennium, I.B. Tauris (London, 2002)

CONTENTS

Chapter 1

An Overview of the Region's Financial Markets

1.1 Financial Deepening

Although the region's financial markets have gained added depth and sophistication in the last few years, nevertheless they remain relatively less developed. They are generally not fully engaged with the region's private sectors, especially SMEs and family businesses, and have lagged behind other emerging markets in resource mobilization and the promotion of healthy economic growth.

It is estimated that in 2014, 80% of the adult population in the MENA region did not have access to formal financial services at a time when eight in ten had mobile telephony. The bottleneck is on the supply rather than the demand side. Financial services providers-who already reap profits from retail and corporate lending, and enjoy risk free exposure to their respective governments, have little incentive to serve the lower end of the market. This, however, is where the majority of the Arab World's population lives, and affording them greater economic opportunities is a priority of governments across the region.

Figures issued by the World Bank show that only 5.6% of adults above 15 years old in the MENA region borrowed money from a bank or another type of financial institution in 2014, almost half the global average of 10.7%. Borrowing from financial institutions excludes the use of credit cards. The World Bank defines a formal financial institution as a commercial bank, credit union, cooperative, post office or microfinance institution. The MENA region's share of adults who borrowed money in 2014 was lower than that of the Euro-zone (15.8%), the developing countries of Europe & Central Asia (12.4%), the developing countries of Latin America & the Caribbean (11.3%), the developing countries of East Asia and the Pacific (11%), South Asia (6.4%) and the developing countries of Sub-Saharan Africa (6.3%).

On a country basis, 15.6% of adults in Lebanon borrowed money from banks or financial institutions in 2014, reflecting the highest share among countries in the MENA region. Jordan followed by 13.6, Tunisia (8%), Egypt (6.3%), the Palestinian territories and Iraq (4.2% each), Algeria (2.2%) and Yemen (0.4%). On a gender basis, 7.1% of males and 4.1% of females in the MENA region who are 15 years or older borrowed money from a bank or another type of financial institution at the end of 2014 relative to 5.8% and 3.1%, respectively, at the end of 2011.

The financial crisis of 2008 – 2009 has produced a wave of regulations to make the world's financial system safer. Banks worldwide are required to hold more capital. They are being pushed out of riskier areas of activities, especially trading of financial instruments such as derivatives, while asset management has been growing much faster outside the banking sector than within it. At the same time all sorts of payment technologies (internet and mobile) are springing up with the potential of cutting banks out of the process. This does not mean that banks are about to fade away, only that their relative weight in the financial system is diminishing as other financial institutions proliferate and grow. Indeed, that is largely what regulators intend. They want to see banks shrink and welcome the transfer of risky assets to other parts of the financial system.

The lack of substantial debt market across a very large and wealthy part of the world economy, from Africa and the Middle East to Pakistan, Iran and ex-Soviet states, also plays a key role in the serious imbalance in world financial markets. While stock market capitalizations are broadly commensurate with GDP shares (with the US accounting for about 25% of world GDP and 25% of world stock market capitalization), bond markets are unbalanced. The US alone accounts for more than 40% of the global bond market, while the US and EU together represent about two–thirds of the global government debt market. In the US and the EU, government debt typically averages around 50% to 60% of GDP.

The very small debt market in the Arab region reflects first the lack of government debt (especially in the GCC where government budgets enjoyed substantial surpluses in the past few years before turning into deficits with the recent decline in oil prices in mid 2014). Secondly, the traditional use of bank finance, thirdly local preferences (relating also to the question of Sharia compliance) and, lastly, the difficulty in creating a corporate debt market in the absence of a meaningful government securities market and benchmark.

However, even without taking into account the question of Sharia compliance, this is very similar to the situation across Asia, excluding Japan. Japan has a very large government bond market although there is little international trade in this market, which is largely held by domestic institutions. But across other countries, many have low government deficits and debt levels (or like Hong Kong with no debt at all) and most of the government and corporate funding requirements are financed through the banking sector.

Funding sources in the MENA Region are still predominantly channeled through the banking system, with equity and fixed income markets playing a marginal role. While the world's financial markets show on average a balanced structure of bank assets, stock market capitalization and debt securities, the capital mix in the region is heavily skewed towards bank assets with a share of 58.8%, equities around 34% and debt securities (bonds and Sukuk) 7.2%. According to the IMF, total financial assets of the region stood at $4,097 billion in 2014, of which $2,405 billion were banking assets, $1,392 billion stock market capitalization and $300 billion bonds and Sukuk.

The total size of capital markets in the MENA region was equivalent to 104.8% of the region's GDP in 2014. The MENA region accounted for 6% of total bonds, equities and bank assets in Emerging Market economies, constituting the second lowest share after Sub-Saharan Africa at 2.6%. Further, bank assets in the MENA region accounted for 6% of Emerging Market bank assets, also representing the second lowest share among emerging economies, higher than only Sub-Saharan Africa at 1.8%.

Also, the stock market capitalization of MENA economies accounted for 9.9% of Emerging Market capitalization in 2014, higher than only Sub-Saharan Africa. Further, debt securities in the MENA region accounted for 2.1% of total debt securities in emerging economies, constituting the lowest share across emerging markets. In 2014, the MENA region accounted for 1.6% of global bank assets, 1.8% of global stock market capitalization, and 0.2% of fixed income markets in the world.

Governments and state owned enterprises have so far dominated primary issuance in the bond and Sukuk market, accounting for 60% of the total. Bank credit to public sector institutions came to an average of 18% of the total in 2014, compared to averages ranging between 4% and 10% in other regions. The average loan to deposit ratio for the MENA region, stood at 77%, the second lowest among all regions of the world.

1.2 Stock Markets

Stock markets of the UAE and Qatar have recently been upgraded to emerging market status, which together with Egypt are the only three Arab countries that have selected listed companies featuring in the Morgan Stanley Capital Index for Emerging Markets (MSCI EM). Morocco and Jordan were downgraded from the emerging market status to join the remaining Arab countries as frontier markets.

Since its founding in 1954 and until mid-2008, the Saudi Stock Exchange had been inaccessible to international investors. Starting in August 2008, however, the country's Capital Markets Authority allowed indirect foreign ownership through total return swap contracts, also known as participatory notes. Investors in these notes do not receive voting rights and are exposed to counter-party risk (swaps are sold through licensed brokers only), potentially reducing their appeal to foreign institutional investors.

Saudi Arabia has opened its stock market to direct investment by foreign financial institutions in the second half of 2015. The opening of the Saudi stock market is a major positive development for the region's capital markets. The total capitalization of MENA stock markets was around $1.4 trillion in 2014, with Saudi Arabia accounting for 33% of the total. The regional average daily liquidity was around $3 billion, of which Saudi Arabia represented 72%. With over 169 listed companies, the kingdom's stock market offers a diversified sector base to international investors. Furthermore, the only stock market in the region that provides exposure to the petrochemical sector is the Saudi market.

In 2014, foreigners owned just 1.2% of the Saudi stock market via swaps, compared to around 8% in the other regional stock markets that are open for foreign investors. After the opening of the Saudi market, and assuming foreign ownership reaches a level similar to other regional equity markets that are open to international investors such as UAE and Qatar, we could see up to around $35 billion of incremental foreign inflow versus the approximately $4 billion that foreigners have accumulated since indirect ownership first became available.

Now that the direct trading restrictions by foreign investors have been removed, the prospect of Saudi Arabia joining MSCI Emerging Markets has become a reality, albeit unlikely before 2017. If promoted, the weight of Saudi Arabia in the EM index is estimated to be 4%, using GCC country weights in the MSCI GCC index as a proxy, and the incremental fund inflows due to eventual MSCI EM promotion could reach up to $10 billion. The combined weight of the MENA region in the MSCI Emerging Markets could then rise to around 3%, from its current level of 1%, putting the region ahead of countries like Indonesia and Thailand.

Saudi Arabia is following a model similar to China when it first opened its bourse to foreign investors. Only qualified institutional investors will be awarded licenses to invest based on three factors: foreign institutions would need to have at least $5 billion of assets under management globally, each institution could own no more than 5% of a Saudi listed Firm, and the total foreign ownership in any company should not exceed 10% of its value.

Foreign investors are facing a clash of investment culture when joining the region's capital markets in terms of transparency, governance, liquidity, regulations, absence of market makers, and prohibition of stock lending or short selling thus greatly restricting portfolio risk management.

Investor relations is little developed or understood except by the largest most global institutions of the region. Several listed companies still publish their quarterly results only in Arabic. While we have equity research on few listed companies, however, most of them are not up to international standards, and not all actively traded companies are regularly covered. Local/regional investment banks are either small or non-existent and have not allocated enough resources to the equity research function.

The total values of initial public offerings (IPO) in the region has remained relatively small, not exceeding $36 billion in the ten year period 2005-2014, compared to $2.5 trillion globally. IPO efficiency, defined as the ratio of IPO value to GDP, has been low during this period, less than 0.5% in the UAE and 0.2% in Saudi Arabia, the two countries where we had most of the IPOs and close to zero in other Arab countries. By comparison, IPO efficiency for Turkey and Malaysia were higher at 1.1% and 6.4% respectively. Even if non-oil GDP is used, it will not alter the relative standings.

Listing rules, valuation methods of IPOs, poor liquidity in the secondary markets following the IPO, absence of peers against which the listed companies will be compared and concerns regarding loss of management control by family businesses were all factors hindering local listings. Several IPOs of companies from the region have been listed on the London Stock Exchange, these include Hikma Pharmaceuticals, Petrofac, DAMAC, Gulf Marine, and Al Noor Hospitals among others.

The region's stock markets are still dominated by retail investors who account for over 90% of daily trading volume, compared to 50% in other emerging markets and a much smaller percentage in developed markets. Retail investors tend to take a shorter-term approach than institutional investors, basing decisions on news headlines, rumors or price momentum, rather than on valuation and equity research.

Regulations and corporate governance remain a challenge in this part of the world. Of the 32 listed companies rated BBB by Standard &Poor's across MENA, only two companies (Majid Al Futtaim and SABIC) got the highest score on governance, compared to 9.5% of listed companies in other emerging markets.

1.3 Fixed Income Markets

The region's fixed income markets are still in their early stages of development. The outstanding amount of bonds and Sukuk issued by sovereign and corporates (excluding local issuance by central banks) reached a total of $250 billion in 2014, accounting for 8.3% of the region's GDP of $3,000 billion, compared to an average of 40% for emerging markets. Sukuk at $90 billion represented 35% of the total amount of debt outstanding, with issuance coming mainly from the Gulf countries.

Countries like Egypt, Jordan, Lebanon and others, who have been more visible in the bond market, have not issued a single Sukuk. Most of the bonds and Sukuk issues have so far been dollar denominated (70% of total outstanding) targeting mainly foreign investors seeking risk diversification and higher returns. The local currency fixed income markets are still in their infancy in the region, with the Saudi Riyal denominated fixed income issues accounting for 15% of the total.

Trading of bonds and Sukuk in the secondary markets remains limited, reflecting the buy and hold approach of investors. While average daily value of stocks traded in the MENA region has reached $3 billion in 2014, 70% of which in Saudi Arabia, daily trading in fixed income securities did not exceed $100 million. Of the total $296 billion Sukuk outstanding world wide in 2014, sovereigns accounted for 36%. A total of $70 billion worth of Sukuk were issued in 2014, with sovereign issuance close to $30 billion.

The primary government bond market is designated mainly for commercial banks and the social security pension funds while retail investors have no direct access to this market. Sovereign yield curves across multiple durations (one to ten years) have yet to be established in most countries of the MENA region so that proper pricing of risk for private issuers could be done. There is no system in place for market makers to provide firm bid-ask quotes on a continuous basis, delaying the development of secondary market for government securities.

There is little or no foreign investors participation in the region's bond markets compared to a much larger ownership in the equity markets (for example foreigners account for 50% of Amman stock market). Although countries of the region do not put any restrictions on foreign purchases of domestic bonds and Sukuk, ownership by foreigners remains very low. In most MENA countries, central banks act as registrars and central depository agencies, which could be a major deterrent for foreign investors in regional government bonds. Ideally, the registrar and settlement functions for bonds should be moved to an autonomous body, based on international best practice.

The corporate bond market remains small and illiquid. The volume of corporate bond issuance is very low when compared to outstanding loans granted by banks. In general, companies find it easier to resort to banks for financing. Equally important, investors' understanding and appetite for fixed income securities need to be enhanced. There are very few regional investment banks capable to issue, underwrite and place corporate bonds. The region lacks credit rating for small issuers, while listing procedures tend to be cumbersome adding to the cost of issuance.

1.4 Other Constituents of the Region's Financial Markets

The mutual funds industry in the MENA region is still in its early stages of development with assets under management (AUM) as a percentage of the region's GDP accounting for a small 2%, compared to 8% in India, 48% in Brazil and 78% in the USA. AUM of mutual funds in the region as a percentage of bank deposits is also small at 4%, compared to 15% in India, 103% in Brazil and 143% in the USA. This points to a lack of mutual fund penetration. The use of mutual funds as an investment vehicle has a long way to go in most, if not all, countries of the region.

With global assets under management in 2014 of $65 trillion, 50% of which in North America, the MENA region accounted for less than 0.1% of world total. There were around 782 mutual funds investing in the region's capital markets in 2014 including all funds that have the

MENA region or one of its constituent countries as their geographical focus, irrespective where these funds are domiciled. Saudi Arabia had the highest AUM in the region of close to $22 billion, accounting for 35.3% of the total, followed by Morocco (22.6%) and Egypt (18.1%).

Family businesses in the region engage in a diverse range of activities, with a typical pyramid corporate structure, where the founder sits at the top and immediate family members form the executive management. The model has been tried and tested and has helped to make family-owned businesses the most important players in the region since 1940s.

Where many family businesses in the West have diluted their holdings from majority to minority stakes, allowing outside professionals to be in the driver's seat, the region's family businesses have yet to fully adapt to the 21st century global corporate culture. There is still, for example, a strong resistance to relinquishing boardroom control and only a few accept to go public in order not to be subjected to stringent disclosure standards enforced by market regulators.

With its successful International Financial Center and its lifestyle advantages, Dubai has managed to establish itself as the leading financial center in the region. However, other financial centers must not be forgotten. Bahrain, the region's oldest offshore banking center, will try to regain market share, especially in Islamic banking where it has long experience and an established regulatory framework. Qatar largely focuses on its domestic energy sector and its project finance needs and has not yet developed a more international profile. Financial liberalization in Saudi Arabia and Kuwait could also pause serious competition to the region's more established financial centers. However, Only Dubai features among the top twenty financial centers worldwide in terms of contribution of its financial services to GDP, after New York, London, Paris, Chicago, Tokyo, Shanghai, Hong Kong, Singapore, Frankfurt, Zurich and Geneva.

There are close to 20 active Private Equity (PE) firms in the MENA region, the largest is Abraj Capital with $7.5 billion. The total funds raised during the period (2004-2014) by the region's PE firms reached $20 billion, of which $12 billion have been invested, leaving $8 billion as "dry powder". Private equity in MENA was not immune to the financial crisis of 2008-2009. When the crisis started in 2008, PE firms in the region were hardly affected because they scarcely use excessive leverage as a funding method. However, in 2009, fund raising dropped considerably to $726 million raised by 2 funds, from $7.1 billion raised by 18 Funds in 2008.

The most attractive opportunities for PE firms in the region are those where the owners are not interested in selling control of companies that they have built over several years but instead, they are looking for hands-on partner who can provide Growth capital with a minority stake of 30%-49%. PE firms who can help transform a family business into a professional corporation, help it expand into new markets that it may be unfamiliar with, and provide world-class operating practices would stand a good chance to outperform.

The whole concept of venture capital is that it targets risky startup companies where few will succeed with time, while the majority will fail. However, Arabs are generally risk averse, preferring to invest conservatively and in hard assets like property rather than in digital ventures. They like to show how successful they are by pointing to their latest apartment building or hotel or manufacturing plant. Arabs like Japanese do not tolerate failure. It is socially unacceptable for a new venture to fail and bankruptcy should be avoided at all costs.

Up until recently, there has been a shortage of seed or early stage funding beyond the initial personal/family funds raised by the entrepreneurs. Innovators have typically faced a "harsh desert" after starting work on an initial idea whether in terms of seed funding, help and knowhow and supporting environment. Interim capital has also been missing, what is known in the US as the second and third round funding. However, this is changing with several funding institutions being established in different countries of the region that aim at enabling early stage companies to transform innovative ideas into viable businesses, and to provide second and third stage funding for the successful ones.

The regional banking sector was not much affected by the global financial crisis of 2008-2009, and had escaped much of the damage that hit elsewhere. This was due to a mixture of prudent regulation, concentration of activities on domestic assets and liabilities, adequate loan loss reserves and a well capitalized banking sector. Aggregate Tier1 capital of the Arab-banking sector reached $250 billion at the end of 2014, an increase of 11% on end of 2012 level. Total assets topped $2,405 billion, with a pre-tax profit of $40 billion. The banks' average return on assets stood at 1.73%, average return on equity of 16.23% and their average capital adequacy ratio at 10.66%. Total assets of GCC banks ended 2014 at $1,250 billion, accounting for more than 50% of Arab banks' total assets.

The most immediate impact of lower oil prices on GCC banks will be felt on the liability side, notably reduced deposit inflows from large government and government-related entities. Direct exposures of banks to GCC governments are limited but, depending on the policy responses, a sustained drop in oil prices could also have pronounced negative effects on public spending, confidence and economic growth. Any immediate impact on asset quality is expected to be low due to the fact that the GCC credit cycle is still in its early stages.

While commercial banks in the region remained generally profitable during the global financial crisis and the uprisings that took place in several Arab spring countries in 2011-2012, the region's leading investment banks experienced tough times. Global Investment House of Kuwait, Shuaa Capital of Dubai, EFG Hermes of Egypt, National Investor of Abu Dhabi, Gulf Finance House in Bahrain among others all suffered major declines and few of them came close to shutting down.

Going forward, the business model of universal banking is expected to take hold where the region's commercial banks will either acquire investment firms, or as many have already done, establish their own investment banking units. Those who want to maintain their autonomy as investment banks may choose to merge with another IB in the region or raise more equity, concentrating on one aspect of the business, e.g. issuance of Sukuk, regional asset management, IPOs, etc.

CHAPTER 2

Stock Markets in the Region: From "Frontiers" to "Emerging" Markets Status

2.1 Introduction

Public companies have been the locomotives of capitalism since they were invented in the mid-19th century. They have installed themselves at the heart of the world's largest economy, the United States before spreading around the world replacing older forms of corporate organization such as partnerships, and newer rivals such as state-owned enterprises. Russia rejected five-year plans in favor of stock-market listings and Wall Street banks abandoned cozy partnerships in favor of public equity: Goldman Sachs, the last big holdout, went public by the end of the last decade.

Public companies triumphed because they provided three things that make for durable success: limited liability, which encourages the public to invest, professional management, which boosts productivity, and "corporate personhood", which means business can survive the removal of a founder. Public companies produce annual reports, hold shareholder meetings and are subject to regulatory authorities. Unlisted private companies by comparison operate behind a veil of secrecy.

The economic crisis in 2008, which led to a meltdown in global equity markets, affected the equity markets in the MENA region as well. Despite sustained public spending by oil-rich GCC economies to offset the fallout from the global economic slowdown, business and investor sentiment suffered due to lack of liquidity in equity markets. A decline in trading volumes and negative investor sentiment strained stock markets, causing many local companies to cancel or defer IPOs. Liquidity shrank further, as banks in the region reduced lending for stock purchases due to high probability of defaults. This resulted in high provisions for impaired stock loans. Total number of listings dropped significantly to 16 in 2009 from 45 in 2008, while total proceeds eroded to about $1.2 billion from $12.4 billion during the same period.

The MENA IPO market performed vigorously during 2014, raising $11.5 billion from 27 IPOs. This was the market's best performance in term of proceeds after the 2008 economic crisis when it had raised $12.4 billion from 45 issues. However, the average deal size in 2014 was significantly higher than that of 2008 by 66%.

The strength of the IPO market continued in the first half of 2015, with $2.5 billion raised, with the banking and industrial sectors being the most active. We expect the momentum to continue in the coming few years, driven by MSCI's upgrade of Qatar and the UAE to Emerging Markets status and the opening up of Saudi stock market to foreign institutional investors starting in the second half of 2015.

2.2 Structure and Sectoral Composition

Most if not all-Arab countries have stock markets; some are still in their early stages of development with few companies listed and traded, while others are more developed, increasingly gaining depth and significance. The embryonic nature of the region's stock market is signaled by the fact that most are still considered "frontier" markets. Only Egypt, UAE and Qatar have the "Emerging" market status, with selective listed companies featuring in the Morgan

Stanly Emerging Market Index (MSCI EM). Both UAE and Qatar stock markets joined the MSCI EM index in May 2014, while Jordan and Morocco were downgraded from the emerging market status to the frontier status in November 2008 and December 2013 respectively.

Most regional stock markets do not provide instant clearing, have yet to allow short selling, and do not offer derivatives or complex financial products considered instrumental for hedging and risk management. Frontier markets tend to be more thinly traded, with average daily trading volume not exceeding $50 million, making it challenging for large institutional investors to enter and exit these markets when needed. Frontier markets also have lower market capitalization to GDP ratios, restrictions on foreign ownership, and cumbersome trading and settlement procedures.

Companies included in the emerging market indices should have a minimum average investible market capitalization of $100 million. As a comparison, the value of all the freely traded shares of listed Egyptian companies featured in the MSCI EM index is equivalent to the market capitalization of a single firm in the US: Burger King.

The combined capitalization of Arab stock markets reached $1,392 billion by the end of 2014, equal to that of Hong Kong. The largest market in the region is that of Saudi Arabia, capitalized at $453 billion, accounting for 65% of the country's GDP (Chart 1). UAE (Dubai and Abu Dhabi) comes next at $196 billion accounting for 48% of GDP. Qatar is the third largest Arab stock market capitalized at $154 billion (76% of GDP), followed by Kuwait at $103 billion (58% of GDP) and Egypt at $74 billion (23% of GDP).

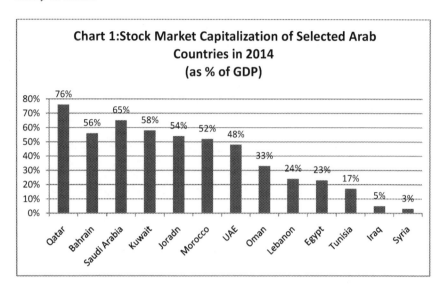

The number of listed firms on the region's exchanges is still small with less than half of the companies listed being actively traded. Similarly market turnover is low except in Saudi Arabia with average daily volume of shares traded in 2014 of around $2.3 billion, but activity is often concentrated in speculative stocks. Average daily trading volume picked up in Dubai in 2014 to reach $294 million, in Abu Dhabi ($112 million), in Qatar ($206 million), and in Egypt ($100 million). Daily market turnover is way below these levels in all other Arab stock markets (table 1).

Table 1
Performance of Selected Arab Stock Markets: 2014

Country	Market Capitalization ($ billion)	2013 % Change of Market Index	2014 % Change of Market Index	Average Daily Volume Traded ($Million)	P/E	P/B	Dividend Yield (%)
Saudi Arabia	453	25.5%	-2.4%	2,351	15	2.0	3.6
Qatar	154	24.2%	18.4%	206	10	1.5	4.4
Abu Dhabi	116	63.1%	5.6%	112	14	2.1	4.1
Kuwait	103	27.2%	-13.4%	98	16	1.3	3.5
Dubai	80	107.7%	12.0%	295	11	1.6	4.1

Egypt	74	22.6%	31.6%	100	13	1.6	2.1
Morocco	53	-2.6%	5.6%	50	14	1.2	4.7
Jordan	22	5.6%	4.8%	17	14	1.3	3.9
Bahrain	22	17.2%	14.2%	1	10	1.0	4.5
Oman	18	18.6%	-7.2%	19	10	1.5	5.0
Lebanon	10	-1.6%	1.7%	N.A	6	1.0	4.2
Palestine	11	13.4%	-5.5%	N.A	12	1.5	3.5
MSCI Arabia	238	27.7%	6.0%	N.A	17	2.0	3.5

The main reason for the low turnover is the thinness and illiquidity of the markets. Only 5% to 30% of the capital of listed firms is typically freely floating. Large families, governments, and public sector institutions (such as social security and pension funds), tightly hold most of the shares. Roughly, one third of the Saudi market's capitalization is owned by the government (including the public pension fund), and another one third is in strategic holdings by founding families. The same applies in varying proportions elsewhere in the region. So despite the firm commitment of governments in the region to reduce their involvement in economic activities, they ended up acting as business partners in what has become known in the region as government capitalism.

The other key category of shareholders in the region is the wealthy families. The top 10 families own 25% of listed companies in Bahrain, 40% in Kuwait and 58% in Qatar. Bearing in mind the concentrated ownership and the small share of stocks available to be traded, it is not surprising to see that trading is dominated by retail investors, driven mainly by rumors and herd mentality, which explains the speculative nature of these markets.

Most of the region's stock markets are open to foreign investors, albeit in varying degrees. Morocco, Tunisia, Lebanon, Egypt and Jordan do not put any restrictions on foreign ownership, while in Bahrain, foreigners' account for just over half of market capitalization. In the UAE, Qatar and Oman foreigners account for 25% of ownership, while the percentage is estimated to be less than 5% in Kuwait, and Saudi Arabia. There are legislated limits specifying that foreigners cannot own more than 49% in listed companies in the UAE and 25% in Qatar. Once these limits are reached no additional ownership would be allowed. These limits have been on the rise in the two countries after joining the MSCI EM Index. The Emirates have recently introduced a companies' law that allows the UAE cabinet to issue a resolution permitting firms in certain sectors to increase the amount of capital available to overseas investors.

Although retail investors dominate trading in the region's stock markets, nevertheless the presence of institutional investors has been on the rise with banks, mutual funds, pension funds, insurance companies and foreign investors assuming a bigger role. In Oman for example, banks dedicated 10% of their portfolio investment to the Muscat stock market. Mutual funds are particularly important in Saudi Arabia, where most banks have established funds targeting the local equity market.

In terms of sectoral composition, banks and financial institutions dominate the region's stock markets, accounting for 51% of S&P index for MENA, compared to 36% in Africa and 16% in Latin America. In the GCC markets, banks and financial institutions account for more than 40% of market capitalization. Except in Dubai, financial institutions have the largest market share and often have the largest trading value too. Real estate companies constitute the second largest sector followed by services (telecom, utilities, media etc.), industry and insurance. In the Saudi stock market, the petrochemical sector is the second largest after banking and finance sector.

The region's stock markets are highly concentrated, with the largest five companies accounting for 40% to 50% of market capitalization. In Saudi Arabia for example, SABIC, Rajhi Bank, Saudi Telecom, Samba Bank and Saudi Electricity Company jointly account for 45% of total market capitalization.

The regulatory environment has improved considerably in the past few years. With the exception of Bahrain, all countries now have formally independent regulatory and supervisory capital market authorities (CMAs) overseeing markets and market players. Both international and domestic factors led to a regional frenzy of legislation and regulation, and the region has been following global trends of adopting corporate governance principles. However, more needs to be done to bring markets of the region up to international best practice in terms of disclosure, governance and transparency.

2.3 Performance and Valuation

Arab stock markets increased by 1.8% in 2014, compared to 21.2% in 2013, 3.6% in 2012 and -12.7% in 2011. After recording an increase of 23.5% in 2007, the S&P Pan Arab composite index lost 51.6% during the world financial crisis of 2008 before correcting higher in 2009 and 2010 by 13.6% and 11.4% respectively (table2).

Table 2
Performance of Arab Stock Markets: 2006-2014

	2006	2007	2008	2009	2010	2011	2012	2013	2014
S&P Pan Arab Composite Index	-36.6%	23.5%	-51.6%	13.6%	11.4%	-12.7%	3.6%	21.2%	1.8%

Egypt was the best market performer in the region in 2014, rising by 31.6%, followed by Qatar (18.4%), Bahrain (14.2%) and Dubai (12%). The markets of Jordan and Lebanon ended the year up 4.8% and 1.7% respectively. Saudi Arabia, Palestine, Oman, Kuwait and Iraq closed the year in negative territories. Falling oil prices with Brent crude dropping towards $50 a barrel undermined confidence in the GCC stock markets and contributed to their weak performance in 2015. In comparison, MSCI world index was up 4.1% in 2014, and the MSCI EM index was down 4%. Japan was up 8.8% for the year in yen terms, the US (S&P 500) up 13.1%, and Germany up 3.9%.

The good performance of UAE's stock markets in 2014 and 2013 came on the back of good news, vastly improved economic fundamentals and strong inflow of capital. The Emirates received a boost when MSCI upgraded the UAE to emerging market status along with Qatar. Moreover, the real estate sector experienced a decent recovery, both in terms of transaction volumes and property prices, which recorded increases of 30% and 20% respectively. Furthermore, Dubai's successful bid to host the World Expo 2020 gave an added boost to investors' expectations.

Both Saudi Arabia and Qatar enjoy some of the strongest economic fundamentals in the in the world and their markets have barely scratched the surface of their potential. Kuwait continues to be the regional laggard, as its potential remains constraint by political disagreements.

Egypt did well despite the internal power struggle and political uncertainty. The removal from power of the first Islamist regime by the end of June 2013, gave the country's stock market a big boost. The market index surged 55% in the second half of 2013, outpacing the UAE during this period and rose by 31.6% in 2014. Jordan's performance came relatively weak, underpinned by surrounding regional instability, influx of Syrian refugees and a widening budget deficit. Lebanon's economic imbalances and political divisions, as well as, regional uncertainties added to the country's high risk and led to the weak performance of the stock market in 2013 - 2014.

Liquidity returned to the regional markets in 2013 and 2014. UAE saw the greatest improvement in daily trading volumes, with Dubai averaging $295 million a day in 2013 and 2014 compared to around $25 million in 2010 - 2011. Other markets such as Qatar and Oman recorded an increase in their trading volumes as well. With an average of $2.3 billion of stocks traded daily in 2014, the Saudi stock market remains the region's most liquid one.

Even with the excellent performance of the Gulf stock markets in 2013 and the generally good performance in 2014, the region's stock markets remain reasonably valued compared to other emerging markets with price earning multiples (P/E) below 15, price to book (P/B) below 1.6 and dividend yield above 3.5%. These indicators compare favorably well with an average P/E for S&P 500 of 17.2 and 19.8 for MSCI EM index.

Prices of listed companies have recovered from deeply discounted levels, but the move up was quick and substantial. Share prices are at levels where earning growth and other fundamental factors will take on greater importance in keeping investor sentiment positive.

2.4 Oil Markets and GCC Equity Markets

Historically, the correlation between oil prices and stock market indices of the GCC countries held strong up to the global financial crisis of 2008-2009. While oil prices surged during the period 2010-mid 2014, stock market indices were down by 24%. The disconnection between oil prices and stock market prices was due to several factors such as Dubai Financial Crisis, Arab Spring and tighter credit conditions, which limited the growth of the banking sector. The correlation between oil markets and equity indices rose above 60% well into 2015.

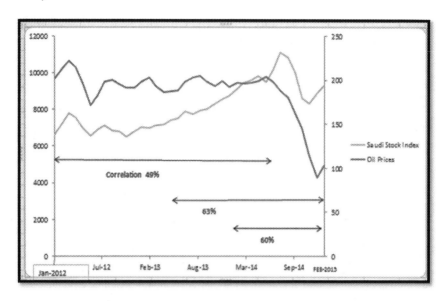

With GCC reserves totaling over $2.8 trillion, the key economies command an expenditure coverage ratio of over three times based on 2014 estimated expenditure figures. This should provide sufficient comfort and cushion to future government expenditure programs and allay investor fears about regional prospects that are predominantly fueled by government expenditure programs.

GCC governments should consider the recent fall in oil prices as a wake up call to accelerate their diversification programs, enhance their revenue streams by introducing indirect taxation, curtail inefficient subsidies and align their policies to achieve fiscal discipline. GCC governments boast stronger credit profile and they should leverage this opportunity to develop their debt markets. Gulf currencies that are pegged to US dollar are insulated from currency turmoil that wreaked havoc in emerging markets during financial crises.

2.5 Role of the Region's Stock Markets in Mobilizing Investments

There is evidence suggesting that raising equity has not been so far a key strategy for listed firms and both listed and non – listed firms continue to rely on retained earnings and bank lending to finance growth and expansion. Most private companies in the region are family owned or family controlled, and owners are unwilling to relinquish control for legacy reasons. Additionally, some families may have unrealistically high expectations regarding the values of their companies and may be unwilling to sell below a predetermined price.

The practice of minority listings demonstrates that firms do use stock markets to raise equity either through IPO or through follow on offering such as rights issues but prefer to retain control and ownership, which limits the use of equity financing. Other reasons for floating shares include better efficiency, increased profile and an opportunity to exit for certain shareholders.

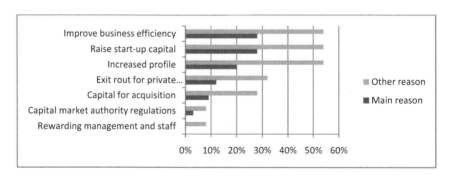

Rights issues allow existing shareholders to contribute to additional equity raised by maintaining their pro-rata holdings in the company. To succeed, rights issues should be made available to existing shareholders at a discount to market prices, allowing them to sell these issues to new investors if they are unable to exercise them.

There are other advantages that going public offers companies, such as deleveraging, greater brand exposure, increased flexibility in future mergers and acquisitions, the potential for lower cost of funding and efficiency gains, opportunity for refinement in corporate governance, and the prospect of an increased range of tools for employee retention. In the GCC, governments have also sometimes used IPOs as a way of redistributing wealth, with subscription restricted to nationals and pricing set at book value rather than market prices through a process of book building. With most governments in the region enjoying financial surpluses, sale of government stakes in companies has not necessarily been driven by the need to raise funds for the budgets.

IPO value by country shows relative concentration reflecting the share of the largest economies in global economic activity. Data for the past decade put the U.S. at the forefront globally in terms of IPO activity. However, in recent years Asia and China in particular have seen more IPOs. In the MENA region, Saudi Arabia and the UAE lead the pack (see table 3). One way to normalize for economic size is to look at the ratio of IPO value to GDP, defined as IPO efficiency. In terms of the proportion of IPOs compared to the size of an economy, Singapore, Malaysia, and Hong Kong score highly. IPO efficiency has been lower in the GCC than in these economies. Even if non-oil GDP is used, it will not significantly change IPO efficiency and would not alter the relative standings.

Table 3

IPO Efficiency	IPO Value ($billion)		IPO Value to GDP (%)	
	2004 - 06	2011 - 13	2004 - 06	2011 - 13
Singapore	13.1	27.6	10.2	9.7
Malaysia	5.0	19.5	3.5	6.4
China	116.5	239.4	5.1	2.9
Norway	16.4	7.1	5.4	1.4
Turkey	4.3	9.1	0.9	1.1
Oman	1.0	0.5	3.2	0.6
UAE	6.0	1.7	3.2	0.5
Saudi Arabia	3.3	1.6	1.0	0.2
Qatar	1.2	-	2.6	-

Source: Bloomberg, IIF.

Looking at capital raised would be one way of assessing the importance of the region's stock markets in mobilizing equity finance for investment. Chart 4 shows that there is a small but rising market for IPOs in the region, with equity raised surging from $7.9 billion in 2006 to $13.5 billion in 2007 and the number of companies going public on the stock exchanges of the region rising from 30 in 2006 to 58 in 2007. However, with the advent of the world financial crisis, the value and number of IPOs in the MENA region dropped to $12.3 billion, corresponding to 41 companies going public in 2008, and receded further to $2 billion in 2009 with only 12 companies issuing shares. During this period, IPOs and Rights issues floated in the Saudi market accounted for more than half the capital raised in the region's stock markets.

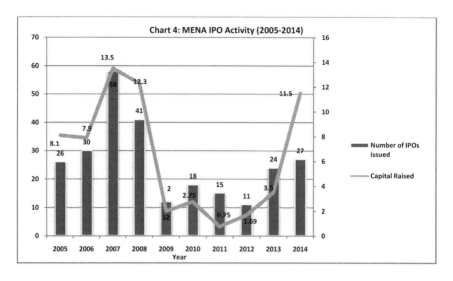

IPO activities in the MENA region rebounded in 2010, with 18 IPOs raising $2.75 billion, an increase of 38% on the capital raised the year before. In the following two years, values decreased dramatically, with the number of IPOs in the region dropping to 11 in 2012 raising $1.69 billion, compared to $750 million raised in 2011 corresponding to 15 issues. The year 2013 saw the amount raised surging by 100% compared to 2012 with 24 IPOs raising $3.5 billion. The first quarter of 2013 witnessed Iraq launching an IPO through Asiacell Communications, the first on the Iraqi stock exchange, raising over $1.27 billion, which was the biggest boost to the total value of IPOs floated during the year. Five IPOs were launched in Saudi Arabia raising $523 million, while two companies went public in Oman raising $180 million. There was one IPO in Qatar for Masaeed Petrochemical Holding Company, a subsidiary of Qatar Petroleum, raising $800 million but was limited to Qatari investors.

North Africa's IPOs came from Morocco and Tunisia with the later issuing 11 IPOs raising $309 million, a drastic increase from 2012 where Tunisia only witnessed two IPOs raising a meager $7.8 million. The other Arab stock markets have not recorded any IPOs activities in the last four years (2010-2014).

The MENA IPO market performed vigorously during 2014, raising $11.5 billion from 27 IPOs. This was the market's best performance in terms of proceeds after the 2008 economic crisis when it had raised $12.3 billion from 41 issues. However, the average deal size in 2014 was significantly higher than that of 2008 by 66% (table 4). In the last few months of 2014, the IPO market witnessed intense activities, mainly led by some big names including the National Commercial Bank of Saudi Arabia (NCB) and Emaar Mall Group, the two companies alone raised $7.6 billion and were over subscribed 23 and 25 times, respectively. The UAE and Saudi Arabia led the MENA region with total proceeds of about $10 billion in 2014. The region's manufacturing sector was the most active in 2014 with five IPOs, followed by the food & beverages, oil & gas and real estate sectors with three IPOs each.

We expect the momentum to continue, driven by MSCI's upgrade of Qatar and the UAE to Emerging Markets, the liberalization and opening up of Saudi stock market to foreign investors, sustained investment in developing social infrastructure, and capacity building to host upcoming global events such as FIFA 2022 in Qatar and Expo 2020 in Dubai. The decline in oil prices has been dragging the equity markets of the GCC down. If this continues, market valuations for the IPOs will not be meaningful and may lead to fewer IPOs being issued.

The top five sectors in 2014 saw the financial sector leading the pact with 32.1%, followed by the real estate sector (15.3%) and the industrial sector (12.3%). The remaining 40.3% was distributed among the other sectors mainly: health care, utilities, retail and insurance.

While new listing appear to have contributed regularly to increased market capitalization, nevertheless, it can be said the MENA stock markets have so far provided a small, at times minute – proportion of the much needed fresh equity capital to listed and unlisted companies.

IPOs in the region tend to be concentrated in a few sectors. There are a number of reasons for this. First, the economic base is relatively narrow. Second, GCC states typically control hydrocarbon resources closely and this sector does not tend to be well represented in regional stock markets. Third, listing rules in some regional exchanges may deter potential IPO candidates for reasons such as concerns regarding loss of management control.

Table 4

Top Initial Public Offerings in the Region ($million)		
Company	Date	Amount
Saudi National Commercial Bank	19/10/2014	6,000
DP World	10/04/2007	4,963
Saudi Telecom	12/16/2002	4,080
Saudi Arabian Mining	06/25/2008	2,467
Saudi Kayan Petrochemical	04/11/2007	1,800
Emaar Malls Group	02/10/2014	1,579
Masraf Al Rayan	12/22/2005	1,133
Deyaar Development	02/27/2007	865.5
Investcom LLC	09/26/2005	778.0
Oman Telecom	05/05/2005	748.1
Air Arabia PJSC	01/22/2007	698.8
Emaar Economic City	07/11/2006	679.9

Source: Bloomberg, IIF

2.6 IPO Pricing and Execution Mechanisms

There are two methods of pricing IPOs: book building or fixed price. Although common in developed markets, book building is still not adhered to in all of the region's stock markets. The common practice had been to bring companies to the market at fixed IPO price. This price is normally based on the company's assets, cash flow and future profitability, as determined by one of the big accounting firms. The regulator would review the valuation method and approve the price per share arrived at by applying this approach. According to the fixed price method, the valuation of the company is divided into a certain number of shares at a nominal price of say 10 Saudi riyals in Saudi Arabia or 10 Dirhams in the UAE. The intention is to benefit retail investors, as institutional investors are restricted from bidding early on for the entire amount they need.

This method was applicable when the majority of listings have been in start-ups and green field companies which made it difficult to assess the true value of a new IPO. There has been as well a general perception that new share offerings by government owned companies is a form of wealth distribution and governments wanted to make sure that a broad number of retail investors would subscribe to the IPOs.

Book building provides a transparent process for the determination of the IPO price using the hard commitments of the investors in the order book as feed back in forming a view on optimal price. The investment bank would come with a price range based on equity research and valuation and would request bids from institutional investors based on various price levels, in effect coming up with a likely demand curve for the offering. The company going public would determine how much it is willing to off-load to the market within this price range (supply curve). A typical IPO execution time table is given in chart 5.

Chart 5: The IPO Execution Timetable

Preparation	Analyst education	Transaction launch	Roadshow	Pricing and Floatation	Aftermarket
15-20 weeks	7 weeks	4 weeks	2 weeks	1 Day	Up to 4 weeks

1

2

3

4

5

6

Preparation

- Business plan/capital structure
- Management and Board
- Audited account and short forms if required
- Cash flow forecasts
- Independent technical reports if required
- Prospectus drafting and other documentation
- Due diligence
- Offering structure
- Discussion and review of listing particulars with regulatory authorities

Analyst Education

- Prepare analyst presentation
- Present it to research analysts
- Flagship investors identified
- Agreeing with Management on announcement day
- Prospectus finalized and presented to regulatory and market authorities

Transaction Launch

- Distribution of prospectus
- Sales force briefed by company
- Announce intention to float
- Research published
- Assess initial demand profile and recommend indicative price range

Roadshow

- Price range set and communicated to the market
- Roadshow launch; One-on-one meetings with key institutions, Group meetings
- Book building and demand profile
- Pricing scenario analysis

Pricing and Floating

- Price determination and share allocation

Aftermarket

- Stable market established
- Inclusion in market index as applicable

Open book building enables an optimal price discovery process balancing supply and demand for the offering. Doubling and tripling of the price when trading starts in the secondary market becomes less likely. For example, two companies who followed the fixed price method when floating their IPOs, Arabian Insurance Cooperative Company listed on the Saudi market in 2008 and Ajman Bank listed on Dubai Financial market the same year, saw their IPO prices surging by 680% and 288% respectively on their first day of trading. The book building method allows for the selection of the highest quality investor base, secures orderly prices when market trading starts, encourages more professional investors to participate and more family businesses would probably list, as they would expect to get the true fair value for their companies.

After the completion of the book building period, the issuer and the book runner will determine the "equilibrium" price and amount of shares to be allocated. Determining this price is a balancing act, not only between demand and supply of the shares in the offering but also between various groups of investors, choosing those who are likely to be long-term holders rather than speculators.

2.7 Building an Equity Culture

It is interesting to note that only 12% of companies who floated shares in the region's stock markets cited an exit route for shareholders as the key driver, particularly in a region where family businesses are dominated by second and third generation members. More than twice this number saw an IPO bringing benefits in terms of improved efficiency and additional growth capital. Other reasons for floatation mentioned include increased profile, benefiting from capital market authority's regulations and rewarding management and staff by allocating shares to them.

To reduce the risk of future investment in the region's stock markets, more needs to be done in investors' education. Information on listed companies should be made available to the average investor in a timely manner and in a way where the small investor can understand it. Information on prices, trading volumes and basic background information on listed companies are readily available, what is missing are credible equity analysis to come up with buy, hold or sell recommendation on the most actively traded companies.

Companies in the region are not comfortable giving information to equity analysts. It is not a common practice for the CEO or CFO of listed companies to talk about their future plans and prospects of profits with research analysts. With the exception of few large banks and industrial conglomerates, corporate ratings are virtually non-existent in the region, there are no local or regional specialized agencies that deal with debt and equity ratings. IPO ratings are practically non-existent as well, and the financial media in the region still lacks depth and sophistication.

Disclosure and accounting practices have improved considerably but are not yet up to international standards across the board. Huge deals still take place without full disclosure and few insider-trading deals go undetected. Family companies who went public refuse to change the paternalistic approach of managing the business.

Not all countries have put in place a code for corporate governance for listed companies, and among those who did, some do not enforce compliance of such a code. Investors have a choice where to invest and issuers have a choice where to list. Sophisticated investors and well run family businesses are always attracted to invest and list in the appropriately regulated market, where minority rights are protected, and codes of proper governance are enforced.

Increasingly more small and medium size enterprises (SMEs) worldwide are turning to the capital markets to raise cash. Various stock exchanges are positioning themselves to help SMEs meet at least part of their financing requirements through IPOs. In May

2013, NYSE Euronext launched EnterNext, a marketing initiative to raise the profile of the SMEs segment of the main market, along with Alternext, the traditional market for smaller firms.

Stock exchanges in the MENA region should also start courting small firms with a view to rebuilding new listings. Bank lending to SMEs in the region has been limited, despite official urging, and interest rates for small business loans are persistently higher than for big ones. Government seeks to lure banks to lend more to SMEs through providing cheap funding. However, it is not cheap funding that banks lack but the capital needed to back the risky loans to SMEs. Stock exchanges should provide all the legal and technical support needed to lure SMEs to issue IPOs on the SMEs segment of the main market, especially for profitable or higher growth SMEs.

There are many closed companies in the region, mainly family owned or private partnership companies who could be groomed to become public shareholding companies. Private partnerships lack the ingredients of limited liabilities: partners could lose everything they owned if the business failed. Capital market authorities and the region's stock exchanges are called upon to serve as incubators for closed companies and to prepare a selective group of them to become publicly listed companies. Many of the closed companies need to be restructured and monitored for several years before making the transition. Once they put in place rigorous systems of corporate governance and financial reporting and show good profitability and better leverage indicators, they could then be taken public. The process will give a much-needed push to the fledgling IPO markets in the region.

Several companies listed on the region's stock exchanges have been reporting successive losses for several years in a row. This should not be allowed to continue. It will not only dampen market indices but would also impact negatively investors' confidence. Regulatory authorities should either force these companies to change their senior management and board composition or have them delist, but keeping the door open for them to regain their stature as public companies once they become profitable. A key performance indicator for the region's regulators should be their success in forcing public companies to regain profitability or delist.

As increasingly more of institutional investors (pension funds, mutual funds, insurance companies, hedge funds etc.) become dominant, including the professionally managed foreign funds, this would greatly boost depth, add liquidity and help build an equity culture in the region's capital markets. Liquidity is a key dimension for survival and growth of the brokerage industry and can be a key input for foreign investment. It is also an important factor for including MENA markets in global indices like the MSCI Emerging market index.

There is a need to provide more tools for risk management. MENA stock markets are inherently more volatile than their emerging market peers primarily due to their nascent stage of development. Hence, managing this risk or volatility is a key underpinning for the entry of institutional investors. A buy and hold environment may not enable this. Availability of broader tools like derivatives (options and futures) can provide the needed tools for managing this volatility. Derivatives have bad reputation in the region primarily because of their debilitating effect in the Global Financial Crisis. However, a good tool in the hands of a bad person does not make the tool bad. Proper checks and balances can make this serve the original purpose for which it is invented, to hedge risk and protect downside.

The gradual integration of the MENA exchanges would primarily entail aligning the policies and regulations under which the region's bourses operate. Each bourse would remain independent and continue to be regulated by local authorities, but rules and regulations would be standardized across all bourses. Such an initiative would presumably represent an interim step towards an ultimate region-wide consolidation.

CHAPTER 3

Bond Markets:
An Untapped Source of Funding

3.1 Introduction

A lesson learnt from the 1997 – 1998 Asian Financial crisis and the 2008 – 2009 world credit crisis is the importance of having a deep and liquid domestic bond market which can reduce the corporate sector's reliance on financing through short–term bank debt.

The advantage of raising medium to long–term money in the region's bond markets is to diversify sources of funding and reduce the corporates' overdependence on borrowing from banks. Also in low interest rate situations, corporates can lock in low interest rates for say a five year period and have the advantage to repay the principle amount borrowed in one bullet repayment or to refinance it with another bond on the maturity date. Equally important, issuance of bonds will enhance financial transparency and improve the corporate image of the issuer. At the same time, deep and liquid domestic bond markets will open a new asset class that would help repatriate at least part of the region's high savings, currently invested in assets of developed markets.

The development of local currency bond market represents a vital investment in the economy. Even in the absence of pressing need among governments, especially those of the Gulf countries, to borrow, the creation of a debt market is an important milestone on the road to development. Bonds help central banks manage liquidity and provide instruments to the banking system to mange risk in an effective manner. A developed bond market also promotes transparency and accountability because those issuing bonds are doing it based on their own credit outstanding, as there is usually no collateral to back up the bonds in case of default.

Bond financing offers several benefits to project developers. Bonds are drawn down in full at the start and repaid in full at maturity. Removing the burden of making repayments in the early stages of a project where cash flows tend to be negative can be extremely helpful. In the MENA region bonds peaked at 5% of the project finance market in 2006 and fell to virtually nothing when the world financial crisis took hold in 2008, before recording a gradual uptrend thereafter.

Banks in the region are operating close to the 80% mark of their loan to deposit ratios. Pressure will remain on banks to raise medium and long-term funds by issuing bonds. This will help reduce the mismatch between their sources of funds (mainly short term deposits) and the longer-term nature of their lending.

3.2 Annual Issuance of Bonds

Global bond issuance reached $8.5 trillion in 2014, up 6.25% on 2013 and almost double the level in 2009 (chart 1). Companies have been keen to take advantage of historically low rates that may not last for a long period of time. Apparently investors have been happy to take the extra risk in search for higher returns at a time when short rates were close to zero or even negative. Ten-year government bonds in the US, Europe and Japan have ranged between 1% to 2% during 2009-2014. Many companies were able to borrow at rates that governments would have been pleased to achieve two decades ago.

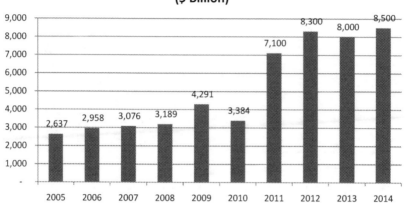

Chart 1 : Global Bond Issuance 2005-2014
($ Billion)

MENA debt capital markets have seen a dramatic rise during the past few years on the back of fiscal reforms, heavy capital spending, rising budget deficits, surge in infrastructural projects, lower yields internationally and cautious bank lending.

After dropping to $15.3 billion in 2008 from $30 billion in the previous two years, bonds issued by both governments and corporate entities in the MENA region surged to a high of $39.7 billion in 2009, before assuming a declining trend dropping to $32.2 billion in 2012 (chart 2). Debt issuance rose to $40 billion in 2014, up from $39.2 billion in 2013, before dropping to $14.5 billion in the first half of 2015, down 46% on mid 2014 level.

Chart 2: MENA Bond Markets Issuance (2003-2014) ($ Billion)

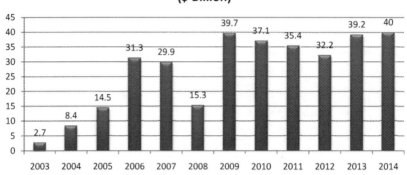

The UAE continued to be the largest issuer of bonds with $14.6 billion issued in 2014, almost 50% of the total for the region. Saudi Arabia came second with $6.2 billion, followed by Kuwait $4.8 billion, Qatar $4 billion, Bahrain $3.5 billion, Lebanon $1.2 billion and Oman $0.7 billion (chart 3). Saudi Arabia issued SR 15 billion ($4 billion) worth of government bonds in the first half of 2015 to help finance its budget deficit.

Chart 3 :MENA Bond Markets: Most Active Issuing Countries (2014)

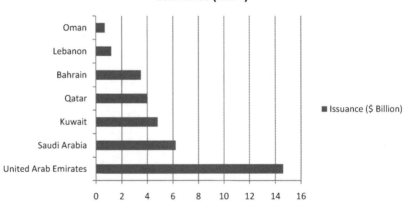

Analyzing the sectoral data for bond issuance, we find that Banks and Government Institutions are among the largest issuers of bonds

40

in the region. For the year 2014, banks were in the lead both in terms of value and volume. A total of 41 bonds were issued in that sector valued at $13.26 billion, followed by government institutions at $9 billion, oil and gas at $5.1 billion, power and utilities at $3 billion, and real estate at $0.6 billion (chart 4). The number of bonds issued reached 88 in 2014, up from 69 in 2009 and 65 in 2011, while total size of bonds issued reached $40 billion in 2014 compared to $31 billion in 2012 (table 1).

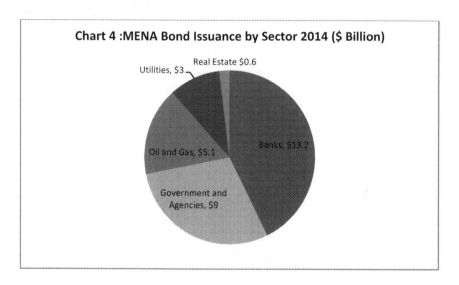

Chart 4 :MENA Bond Issuance by Sector 2014 ($ Billion)

Table 1
Snap shot of MENA Bond Market

	2009	2010	2011	2012	2013	2014
Total Size of bond issues ($billion)	39.7	37.1	35.4	32.2	39.2	40.0
Total No. of bond issues	69	82	65	85	88	88

US dollar denominated issuances comprised 70% of the total amount outstanding by the end of 2014, followed by Saudi Riyal denominated issuances with 15%. Since the majority of MENA bonds are issued in US dollars, then it comes at no surprise that most of the buyers are outside the region. Analysis is difficult since breakdown of distribution by investor category tend to be closely held. Regional issuers sometimes specifically favor international investors at the expense of regional ones for the purpose of establishing their credit standing. In the region, the largest groups of buyers tend to be social security funds and treasuries of commercial banks.

There has been an increase in corporate and quasi–government issuers opting for Reg 144A types of issues, which are regulated under the US securities commission allowing US onshore investors to buy into the issue. Although Reg 144A issuance requires extra disclosure, nevertheless it opens a more diverse funding base as demand for high rating emerging market debt continues to rise.

Lebanon has tapped the international capital markets several times with bond issuance over the past couple of decades, making it the most frequent fixed income issuer in the MENA region. The aggregate Lebanese bond portfolio stood at around $18 billion by the end of 2014, of which $17.5 billion was sovereign and $500 million of corporate bonds mainly for Lebanese banks. Lebanon's debt is largely domestic, with Lebanese institutions and individuals accounting for 88% of total debt outstanding.

3.3 Corporate Bond Markets

The corporate bond markets in the MENA region are still in their early stages of development, with total value of corporate bonds outstanding not exceeding $21.2 billion by the end of 2013, compared to the total capitalization of Arab stock markets of $1,220 billion. Government and quasi government issues accounted for more than 50% of total value of bonds issued during the period 2009-2013 (table 2). Not only primary markets where new bonds are issued are thin, but also the secondary markets for bonds are illiquid. Bond trading makes up a small fraction of total trading in the region's capital markets. Investors, typically treasuries of banks, social security funds and insurance companies tend to hold bonds to maturity. Getting a competitive code on a corporate bond listed could take hours compared to seconds in the Eurobond market.

Table 2

Bond Issuance Breakdown by Issuer Type

	2009		2010		2011		2012		2013	
	No.	Size	No.	Size	No.	Size	No.	Size	No.	Size
Corporate	31	$13.7 billion	38	$15.6 billion	26	$8.3 billion	45	$15.9 billion	46	$21.2 billion
Government	32	$23.2 billion	35	$11.8 billion	30	$17.5 billion	32	$9.0 billion	33	$11.0 billion
Quasi Government	6	$4.9 billion	9	$10.3 billion	9	$9.6 billion	8	$6.1 billion	9	$7.0 billion

Source: Markaz, Kuwait Financial Sector, 2014

The presence of excess liquidity in the domestic banking sector should not be a reason to delay the development of the local corporate bond market. The argument that banks are capable to provide all the capital that corporates need does not always hold. A viable local bond market would provide an alternative source of financing for corporate borrowers, which tend to be of medium to long-term nature and would help reduce their overdependence on borrowing from banks. In the US market, corporates depend on the bond market for more than 60% of their financing requirements compared to less than 9% in the region. The shortage of medium to long-term funds borrowed at fixed interest rates is perceived to be a significant impediment for financing of the region's infrastructure and industrial projects.

While corporate bonds normally cost the borrower less than bank loans, nevertheless certain fees will have to be incurred when issuing bonds. The investment bank charges an underwriting and investment fee of 0.5% to 1% of the total amount issued for high quality bonds.

The underwriting fees for junk bonds could be as high as 3%. Other fees include legal expenses, cost of securing a credit rating for the issuer, registration and custody fees among others. On the average, total cost of issuing a corporate bond could add 0.1% annually to the stated interest on the bond.

Various types of corporate debt securities are available to allow corporations to meet their financing requirements. These include: Commercial Paper, Medium Term Notes (MTNs) and various types of corporate bonds: convertible bonds, callable bonds, straight bonds, Floating Rate Notes (FRNs), Zero Coupon bonds and Contingent Convertible bonds (COCO).

Commercial Paper (CP) is a short-term unsecured promissory note that corporations use as an alternative to borrowing from banks, with maturities ranging from 30 days to 270 days. Interest rates on CPs are quoted on a discount basis. The purchaser pays a discount price and receives the face amount when the paper matures. Interest rates on CP are often lower than bank lending rates and the issuer is not required to provide a collateral because lending is based on the credit standing of the issuer.

Medium term notes (MTNs) are corporate debt instruments with maturities ranging from 9 months to 5 years, mainly issued to support funding requirements of banks. Security firms distribute MTNs for the issuers on a best effort basis, without guaranteeing a price or the amount to be placed for the issuer. MTNs are sold in relatively small amounts on a continuous basis. Because the notes offering are ongoing, they are typically registered with the regulatory authority, which allows a corporation to issue securities up to an approved amount over a specific period of time.

Convertible bonds have a feature that gives the bondholder, the right to convert par amount of the bond into a certain number of shares of the issuer's common stock. The ratio at which the par value is converted is known as the conversion ratio. Suppose that the convertible bond gives the bond–holder the right to convert $1000 par amount of the bond into the issuer common stock at $40 per share. The conversion ratio is therefore 25 to 1. A convertible bond with a conversion price far higher than the market price of the stock generally trade at or close to its bond value, because the bond is not likely to be converted. Conversely, when the share price gets close to the conversion price or exceeds it, the convertible bond begins to trade more like equity, as increasingly more bondholders would opt to convert their bonds into shares.

Characteristics of a Straight Bond

- "Straight" is the term used in the markets to describe fixed coupon Bonds.

- The coupon on the Bond is at a fixed rate, set at the time the Bond is issued and applied throughout its life.

- Coupon is payable annually or semi-annually.

Characteristics of Floating Rate Notes (FRN)

- Interest rates change at intervals specified in the Bond documentation.

- Although the actual rates are not known (except for the current interest period), the basis of the rates is stipulated.

- Coupon = reference rate plus quoted margin, typically a fixed spread over LIBOR, e.g. 3 months LIBOR + 25 b.p.

Characteristics of Zero Coupon Bonds

- Pay no coupon.

- Issued at a discount to the face value.

- Instead of coupon payments, investors look to the appreciation in the Bond value through its life, from the discounted price at issue to the redemption at par value upon maturity.

Callable bonds grant the issuer the right to call the bond, i.e. pay off the debt before maturity. Exercising the call option becomes attractive to the issuer when market rates drop sufficiently below the interest rates on the bond so that refinancing the retired debt at the lower rate becomes feasible. The cost to call the bond includes a call premium, administrative expenses and the fee arising from floating a new issue to refund the existing bond. The call feature is a disadvantage to investors who must give up the higher yielding bonds. Therefore investors generally demand a higher yield from callable bond than from non callable ones for the same issuer and the same maturity.

Contingent, convertible bonds, or cocos, as these instruments are known are a new hybrid of bank equity (the money invested by shareholders, which absorbs any losses in the first instance) and debt (which must be repaid unless a bank runs out of equity). Regulators globally are keen on banks having more equity. This makes bailouts less likely and, if they prove inevitable, less painful for taxpayers. Bankers prefer debt because it lowers their tax bill, and improves both profits and bonuses. Cocos are the compromise.

Cocos take multiple forms, but all are intended to behave like bonds when times are good, yet absorb losses, equity-like, in a crisis. At a given trigger point, when equity levels are so low that bankruptcy threatens, cocos either lose some or all of their value, or get exchanged for shares. Regulators have allowed them to be used in limited quantities to meet increased equity requirements.

Cocos can be described as "pre-funded rights issues", a metaphorical fire extinguisher, however, none of the new generation of cocos has ever been tested. Some worry that coco bondholders could incur losses even as the issuer continues to reward shareholders. Such issues have not stopped investors from piling in, at ever-lower yields. Banks worldwide have stepped up issuance, from nearly nothing in 2010 to $80 billion in 2014.

Bonds rated BBB and above by Standard & Poor's are called investment grade bonds, while those with credit rating below BBB are called speculative/ junk bonds or high yield bonds. Before 1980, most junk bonds resulted from a decline in the credit quality of former investment grade issues known as "falling angels". However, the market for high yield debt (junk bonds) is now huge estimated at $1.8 trillion. Almost half of all the corporate bonds rated by S&P are classified as speculative. America accounts for 57% of this market, Europe (27%) and the rest of the world (16%).

The rise of high yield bonds has been handy for MENA companies in the wake of the financial crisis, as many banks have been seeking to shrink their balance sheets, and have been less willing to offer loans. Historically, companies in the region have been much more dependent on bank finance than their American or European counterparts. Low interest rates have been good for the bond market in another way. They have enabled companies to refinance their debt cheaply, and so pushed back the day when their finances will be squeezed by higher borrowing costs. A few years ago there was a worry that a lot of debt would need to be refinanced in 2014 and 2015, now the refinancing hump will not come until 2020.

A long period of cheap finance makes it less likely that issuers will be forced to default in the short term, and the reduced likelihood of default makes it more attractive for investors to hold bonds. In the wake of Lehman's collapse, the spread (or excess interest rate) on junk bonds rose so far that it implied default on a scale not seen since the Great Depression. But after a brief spike to 13.7% in 2009, the default rate on global high-yield bonds dropped steadily and was just 2.8% in 2014.

Credit Risk	Credit Rating	
	S&P	Moody's
Investment Grade		
Highest Quality	AAA	Aaa
High Quality	AA	Aa
Upper Medium	A	A
Medium grade	BBB	Baa
Speculative/Junk		
Somewhat Speculative	BB	Ba
Speculative	B	B
Highly Speculative	CCC	Caa
Most Speculative	CC	Ca
Imminent Default	DD	Cb
Default	D	C

Investment banks place the bonds with the public either on a best effort basis or on a fully underwritten basis. The fees paid to the underwriter are higher than what the issuer pays the security firm who places the bond on a best effort basis. In an underwritten offer, the issuer knows ahead of time that the whole bond issue will be sold at the price specified in the prospectus. The difference between the price paid by the buyers and the proceeds to the company are the underwritten expenses or gross spreads. Usually close to 20% of the placement revenues go to the lead underwriter who manages the books, while syndicate members get the remaining 80% on a pro–rata basis.

Every bond offering has a prospectus, which gives a detailed analysis of the issuer, its projected cash flow, its credit rating, use of the proceeds, nature of the offering, the interest rate and risk factors. Repayment of the principle, typically take the form of a sinking fund payment or bullet payment upon maturity. The proposed repayment schedule should be consistent with the projected cash flow of the issuer. There are two types of debt covenants usually specified in the prospectus:

1) Those limiting the percentage of long-term debt to total capitalization.
2) Those restricting the short-term debt level.

To protect the investors, a provision requiring the issuer not to acquire additional debt for a stated period of time is needed. Other covenants include merger and consolidation, sale of assets, limitation on distribution of profits, etc.

3.4 Key Issues for Developing the Region's Bond Markets

1. To be able to access the bond market, the issuer needs to get a credit rating, and this in turn means transparency and full disclosure. Bonds do not usually require collateral or guarantees and are issued to companies that have solid financial positions. The number of credit ratings published in the region has increased substantially over the past five years, albeit from a low base.

Table 3
Sovereign Ratings: July 2015

	S&P	Moody's
Kuwait	AA	Aa2
UAE	AA	Aa2
Qatar	AA	Aa2
Saudi Arabia	AA-	Aa3
Oman	A-	A1
Bahrain	BBB-	Baa1
Morocco	BBB-	Ba1
Jordan	BB-	B1
Tunisia	B-	Ba3
Lebanon	B-	B2
Egypt	B-	B3

The need for a proper rating culture in the region is pressing. While countries, and large listed companies issuing bonds have a credit rating (table 3), many firms are still uncomfortable about obtaining one, with all the disclosure and transparency commitments it entails. This must change if they want to issue bonds and reach a wider group of investors.

2. Government bond markets in the region need to gain added depth and breadth. Government bonds with different maturities need to be issued regularly in order to create a yield curve. This would make it easier for arrangers of corporate bonds to come up with the right price for new bond issues in the primary market. Not only would a developed government bond market help to establish a benchmark for pricing of corporate bonds, but also the market yields on these bonds could serve as a reference point for hedging in the derivative markets and as discount rates to value equities and appraise investment projects.

3. A healthy secondary market in bonds is important to mitigate liquidity concerns. It allows investors to buy and sell their fixed income holdings whenever they want at an observable market set price. So far corporate bonds have been concentrated in the hands of few institutional investors that buy and hold these assets till maturity. The availability of trading information is also important for improving liquidity and price discovery. Most bonds are traded not on exchanges but over the counter, and market information (price and quantity traded) is not always available.

The absence of price data in the secondary market creates particular difficulty for institutional investors who are required to mark their portfolio to the market. Likewise trading volume is low. The region accounts for not more than 3.5% of total emerging market trading, and MENA bonds trade less as a share of outstanding issues than bonds from other regions. Factors that affect liquidity and should be addressed include:

- Having sufficient supply of new issues coming to the market regularly,
- Accurate and reliable benchmark yield curve for government bonds,
- Predictable and regular information flow from borrowers,
- Transparency of pricing in secondary markets,
- A set of efficient and safe framework of trading and settlement that reduces transactions costs,
- A sound regulatory and legal environment, and
- A trusted custodian bank.

4. What is missing from the demand side is the advent of institutional and retail demand. Besides a few pension funds in the region, there are hardly any ready and regular institutional buyers of bonds in this part of the world. In most developed bond markets, demand comes from pension funds, insurance companies, mutual funds, banks and corporate treasuries. In the MENA

region, pension funds are still relatively small and have a bias for equities, insurance companies lack the regulation and expertise that would enable them to actively invest in the region's domestic bond markets. Bond mutual funds are still relatively small. This is mainly due to the lack of sophisticated investment tools that limit hedging and with it the need for professional mutual fund management.

5. Several projects across the Middle East are expected to launch bond issues, indicating that the region's capital markets could become a viable source of financing long term projects. So far most projects in the region are funded through bank debt, equity and export credit agencies. That is expected to change as the new Basel 3 banking regulations would force banks to put more of their capital aside for long term loans, making lending to projects less profitable. However, the bond market is a good option for completed projects with proven cash flows to pay the coupons. It is more likely that the majority of project bonds will be first used to refinance bank debt on completed schemes that were funded at peak pricing.

6. The region should develop a market for high yield bonds targeting companies with credit rating below the investment grade. These bonds typically carry a coupon or interest rates much higher than those on government bonds or investment grade corporate bonds. The total size of the high yield bond market globally, the so-called junk bonds, is close to $1.7 trillion. Almost half of all corporate bonds rated by standard & poor's are classified as speculative or junk. Moving down the credit curve is part of the natural development of the bond market. To succeed we need issuers and investors who are interested to tap this market. So far only few high yield bonds were issued in the region. Dar Al Arkan, a listed real estate company in Saudi Arabia rated Ba3 by Moody's issued a $450 million Islamic bond with 11% yield. MB Petroleum, a private Omani oil service company rated B by

Standard and Poor's also sold a $320 million five year bond that carries a hefty coupon of 11.25%. However, not a lot of companies want to sell debt at these prices and lack of local investors also hampers trading volumes in these bonds.

7. Bond issues from the region should be included in global and regional bond indices. Global financial institution J.P. Morgan Chase included Lebanon in its newly issued Middle East Composite Index (MECI). The MECI tracks US dollar-denominated debt issued by sovereign, quasi-sovereign and corporate issuers in 10 countries from the Middle East region. The index includes 61 issuers and 167 issuances with a total market value of $156.5 billion as of December 31, 2013, which represents 73.3% of the Middle East region's $202.9 billion in dollar-denominated debt (bonds and Sukuk). Standard & Poor's and Fitch Ratings each assigned a rating of 'A-' to the MECI, while Moody's Investors Service gave it a rating of 'A2'.

J.P. Morgan Chase indicated that over half of MECI's total market value is not included in any of its other emerging market indices such as the Emerging Markets Bond Index Global (EMBIG) and the corporate Emerging Market Bond Index Broad (CEMBI Broad). Issues in the Middle East do not meet the required criteria in order to be included in the EMBIG, while government-owned entities are not eligible for either of the two indices. The EMBIG includes the external sovereign debt of only Lebanon, Iraq and Jordan, while the CEMBI Broad carries the corporate debt of only the UAE, Qatar, Saudi Arabia, Kuwait, Bahrain and Oman.

A total of $14.5 billion of Lebanon's dollar-denominated Eurobonds, are included in the MECI, accounting for 25.2% of the total sovereign debt included in the index and, constituting the second highest weight after Qatar's (35.4%). Lebanon's weight in the EMBI was 2.6% by the end of 2013.

8. While there are several laws governing debt securities, they tend to identify the process and requirements for dealing with securities as a whole, without specific details on debt securities. One of the areas, which could benefit from clarification, is that of private placement which allows the use of simplified disclosure. A clear differentiation is needed to provide guidance on the level of disclosure and the offering period for a private issuance compared to a public one. Furthermore the definition of qualified investors needs to be updated.

9. The final factor required to make the regional fixed income market take off is expertise. As the region's debt capital markets gain depth, fixed income proficiency is bound to grow. Part of the job of these experts is to educate the regulators, institutions and retail investors in this region about the advantages of having a vibrant and active local currency bond market. It allows for asset allocation to become more sophisticated and funding sources to become more diverse, reducing in the process the dependence on equity markets and bank borrowing to finance future growth and expansion.

CHAPTER 4

Islamic Financial Markets:
The Rising Importance of Sukuk

4.1 Introduction:

The Islamic financial market stood at an estimated $2 trillion in total assets by the end of 2014, covering Islamic commercial banking ($1,600 billion), Sukuk or Islamic bonds ($300 billion), Islamic funds under management ($80 billion) and Takaful (Islamic Insurance) around $20 billion. While Islamic finance represents a very small portion of global financial assets of 1.6%, it is a fast growing segment in many of its core markets with annual growth rates of 15% to 20%. Iran accounts for 40% of the world Islamic commercial banking assets, followed by Saudi Arabia (15%), Malaysia (10%)and UAE (6.3%).

A variety of factors contributed to the remarkable rise of Islamic assets, most importantly the increased awareness of the concept of Islamic finance based on the principles of sharia, which bans interest and puts emphasis on sharing of risk and return. It also restricts investing in virtual assets such as options and other derivative products. The presence of strong institutional establishments provided the much, needed regulatory and supervisory aspects to Islamic finance. The work done by two internationally-recognized standard setting institutions in the fields of Accounting and Regulation, namely the Bahrain-based Accounting and Auditing Organization for Islamic Financial Institutions (AAOIF) and the Kuala-Lumpur-based Islamic Financial Services Board (IFSB), has significantly lowered barriers to entry, and will continue to act as a driving force in the emergence of globally compatible and comparable standards in Islamic finance.

A key component of Islamic banking and finance is that products and services meet specific requirements and have an appropriate audit trail to prove that transactions comply with Islamic accounting. For example, this style of accounting must use the Hijri calendar, which follows the lunar cycle and has 354 days. Interest based charges are not suitable for Islamic banking. Therefore, the method adopted to charge for services is based on fees and could include a pre-determined profit element. Also, the solutions designed for Islamic banking should be compliant with the guidelines provided by AAOIFI. These standards require that accounting practices address the collection and computation of profit and its distribution.

The various components of transaction banking including, liquidity management, payment systems, trade services, etc. all need to be calibrated for Islamic banking. As discussed, all interest-based transactions in conventional banking need to be excluded. The concepts of Ijara (leasing), Murabaha (buying of goods and selling them at a profit) Musharakah (capital contribution and sharing profit or loss on a pro rata basis), or Wakala (investing on behalf of the depositor) are required to be incorporated. This guarantees that all parties are equal stakeholders in case of profits or losses, sharing the inherent risks of the business.

All products and services must be compliant with Islamic banking standards and approved by the relevant sharia boards. In an Islamic mortgage, for instance, a bank does not lend money to an individual who buys a property, instead, it buys the property itself. The customer can then either buy it back from the bank at a higher price paid in installments (Murabaha) or make monthly payments to the bank comprising both a repayment of the purchase price and rent until he owns the property outright (Ijara).

4.2 Sharia and Time Value of Money

Rational individuals factor the price of time and the price of risk in their investments decisions. They try to determine the value of uncertain cash flows at different points in time, i.e., what is a future uncertain cash flow worth today or what is a certain present cash flow worth at some future date. Accordingly, they require a rate of return that will compensate them for the opportunity cost of funds (price of time) and for bearing the risk of investing (the price of risk). The higher the opportunity cost and /or the risks involved the higher the rate of return required.

It is argued by critics that by prohibiting the charging of interest on loans, even when the rate is equal to the expected inflation rate, Sharia denies savers the right to be compensated for the time value of money. Does this imply that Sharia does not recognize the time value of money? If time has no economic value then there is no need to evaluate different investment opportunities-assuming there is no risk. All what it takes is to sum the future cash flows and choose the ones that maximize it.

To answer the question, let us first review the Sharia ruling related to transactions involving riba:

- It is prohibited to charge interest on loans,
- It is prohibited to charge interest or fees for late payment,
- Different commodities of the same group can be exchanged in different quantities on the spot market but cannot be traded on credit on the future market even if quantities are equal,
- A single commodity cannot be exchanged in different quantities whether on the spot or on credit,
- A commodity can be exchanged for a higher deferred price,
- A commodity can be delivered at a future date in exchange of a lower immediate payment.

The most important deduction from the riba classification is the clear distinction between lending and investing. Time has value, but only when it is associated with real economic activities. Accordingly, Sharia recognizes time value in credit sales but denies any compensation for time in loans even to account for the diminishing purchasing power of money.

4.3 The Potential for Islamic Finance

Today, Islamic finance is growing rapidly and there are 600 financial institutions across 75 countries offering sharia-compliant products and services. This provides a window of opportunity to design and provide products and services in tune with the specific requirements of sharia law.

The world's Muslim population is expected to rise from 1.7 billion in 2014 to 2.2 billion by 2030. Additionally, by 2030, the median age in Muslim-majority countries is expected to be 30 while about 29% of the global young population (15-29) is projected to be Muslim, promising a burgeoning middle class. The economies that comprise the organization of Islamic Countries (OIC) region had a combined nominal GDP of $6.7 trillion in 2014 and are estimated to grow at an average nominal pace of 5.4% during the 2015-20 period. With the demand for financial services typically growing faster than income as countries develop from low-income status, there is scope for fast growth of Islamic finance.

Despite this potential, the Islamic finance market is severely underdeveloped. There are only a few Islamic investment banks and they lack the capability in structuring, originating or arranging capital market transactions. The lack of standardization of Islamic finance instruments such as Sukuk and the underdeveloped financial infrastructure required for secondary markets has also discouraged institutional investors from entering Islamic capital markets, leading to a dearth of liquidity. Currently, the top lead arrangers are mostly non-Islamic banks, including the likes of Standard Chartered, HSBC, Deutsche Bank, and Citi to name a few. The fact that international banks are setting up Sukuk programs with the aim of tapping the pool of cash-rich Sharia-compliant investors would deprive Islamic banks of the opportunity to become Islamic finance market builders in their respective markets.

To compound the competition, developed markets including Britain, South Africa, Luxembourg and Hong Kong issued Sukuk in 2014. This could eventually mean that established financial hubs like London, Hong Kong and Singapore may become strong competitors to the current Islamic finance capitals of Kuala Lumpur and Dubai and potentially succeed in using the emerging market OIC savings to invest outside these countries.

Standardization is one of the biggest barriers to the growth of Islamic finance. While the IFSB and AAOIFI, are standard setters promoting increased standardization and harmonization of Sharia products, it is imperative that central banks and regulators adopt and impose these standards and guidelines in addition to ensuring compliance.

Boards of sharia scholars at financial institutions rule on whether activities and products follow religious principles such as bans on interest payments and pure monetary speculation. They are also involved in audits that determine whether the institutions are operating in a compliant manner. At the same time, the scholars are on the payroll of the Islamic banks, which they vet, an arrangement contrary to good governance. Traditionally, scholars have mostly practiced self-regulation, leaving the process open to accusations of conflicts of interest. The growing role of Islamic finance in some national economies is now prompting government watchdogs to pay more attention to the sector.

One of the main problems that have slowed the growth of Islamic finance is that of liquidity management. Islamic Financial Institutions are not allowed to invest the excess balances they have in interest bearing short-term debt instruments such as treasury bonds or commercial paper, or to draw on the interbank market for that purpose. As a result, most Islamic Financial Institutions end up having highly liquid balance sheets with rising liabilities but only limited opportunities to invest on the asset side. For the past few years, Sukuk of short-term maturities have been creating new venues for the placement of funds and as a liquidity management tool.

From April 1, 2015 the UAE central bank have started to accept a wide range of Sukuk as collateral for banks to access its special lending facility. Bahrain's one-week facility is based on a wakalah contract, where the regulator invests cash on behalf of the lender. It is widely expected that the implementation of Basel III and its new liquidity coverage ratio (LCR) will increase offerings of liquidity management instruments while issuers are likely to list more of their Sukuk on exchanges and that some regulators will start to accept Sukuk as collateral for liquidity provisions.

Bahrain and UAE-based Islamic banks have so far held excess liquidity either in cash or monthly offerings of central bank Sukuk, with maturities between three and six months. This placed them at a disadvantage to conventional banks, which have a wide range of interest earning liquidity management options available. Efforts to develop Sharia-compliant liquidity tools are picking up in several Arab countries. These tools will be important for Islamic banks to boost their competitive positions, all the more so, as the pace of growth in Islamic financial services is outstripping conventional banking growth in the region.

Malaysia ranks first in the Thomson Reuters Islamic Finance Development Indicator, which takes into account quantitative development, governance, social responsibility, knowledge, and awareness. Oman and Bahrain rank second and third in the list followed by UAE.

Oman's central bank appointed in 2014 five members to its Sharia board, which will have direct oversight of Islamic banking institutions, similar to the approach taken by regulators in Malaysia, Pakistan, Morocco and Nigeria. By contrast, most Gulf countries practice self-regulation of Islamic financial institutions, leaving Sharia boards in each commercial bank to determine which products are permissible. Bahrain's central bank has a Sharia board that vets its own products. The United Arab Emirates is planning to follow the centralized approach, backing this up with specific legislation, which could help reduce the risk of conflicting rulings from the Sharia boards of various Islamic banks.

4.4 Structure of the Sukuk Market

Sukuk are Sharia compliant bonds backed by real assets, which generate a rent paid periodically to the Sukuk holders in lieu of interest. A holder of Sukuk has not technically lent the issuer money, instead, he owns a nominal share of whatever the money was spent on and derives income not from interest but either from the profit generated by that asset or from rental payments made by the issuer. At the end of the Sukuk's term the issuer returns the principal to the investor by buying his share of the asset. Cynics may point out that there are few differences between these structures and a conventional bond or mortgage in that both provide predictable income to those who make their capital available. Additional legal and financial work is required to structure Sukuk in a way that renders them more of Sharia compliant products.

If a corporation wants to tap the debt market in a sharia compliant way, a special purpose vehicle (SPV) needs to be established. The SPV will issue trust certificates or Sukuks to potential investors and will use the money raised to purchase a rent generating property. The SPV will then rent the property back to the corporation for say a five year period corresponding to the duration of the Sukuk, and will keep the property or the asset in trust for the holders of the Sukuk. The lease rental payments from the corporation to the SPV will exactly match the periodic payments due to the holders of the Sukuk. These rental payments need not be fixed and may be calculated based on six months US dollar Libor plus a margin.

All claims due to the SPV, the special purpose company issuing the Sukuk, including the rent that will fund the periodic payments on the trust certificates are direct, unconditional and irrevocable obligations of the corporation raising the debt. The corporation is also obliged to purchase from the SPV upon the maturity of the lease the asset or the property leased at the agreed exercise price, which will be used for the repayment of the principle to the holders of the Sukuk.

The global Sukuk market is the most vibrant sector of Islamic finance, accounting for 15% of its total assets. The outstanding market for Sukuk issuance has grown considerably in the last 10 years, surging from $11 billion in 2005 to $135 billion in 2012, before dropping by 16% to $111.3 billion in 2013. Sukuk issuance reached $116 billion in 2014 up 4.5% from 2013 level, and the total is expected to exceed $145 billion in 2015 (chart 1).

The bulk of Sukuk issued came from the sovereign issuers, with only $30 billion from corporates. In comparison, conventional bond issuance worldwide rose from $2.6 trillion in 2005 to $8.5 trillion in 2014. The Sukuk market remains tiny compared with the conventional bond market accounting for around 1.4% of total value of the later. Given the low base of total Sukuk outstanding, total issuance is expected to grow at an average rate of 20% annually in the coming five years.

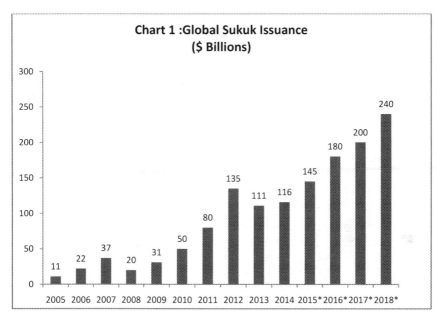

Chart 1 :Global Sukuk Issuance ($ Billions)

*Projection

Despite the drop in the value of Sukuk issued by Malaysia in 2013, the country continued to dominate the global Sukuk market with $60 billion worth of issues, followed by UAE ($20 billion), Saudi Arabia ($11 billion), Turkey ($2.5 billion) and Indonesia ($2 billion).

The Bahrain Monetary Agency (BMA), the country's central bank, issued the first tradable Sukuks in September 2001. Since then the pace of issuance has quickened with Bahrain tapping this market many times, bringing the total value of the Sukuks issued by Bahrain for the period 1996-2014 to the US $14,000 million mark (table 1).

Malaysia was among the early issuers as well with $600 million coming to the market in June 2002. According to the rating agency Standard & Poor's, Malaysia accounted for 66% of the value of all Sukuk issued between 1996 and 2014, followed by UAE (9.8%), Saudi Arabia (8%), Indonesia (4%) and Qatar (3.9%). Corporates from the US, Singapore, the UK, China, Nigeria, Germany and France have tapped the Sukuk market as well. Other global issuers included the International Financial Corporation, the private arm of the World Bank.

Table 1: Breakdown of Global Sukuk issued by country(1996-2014)

COUNTRY	NUMBER OF ISSUES	AMOUNT ISSUED($ MILLION)	% OF TOTAL
Malaysia	2490	324,576.9	66.49%
UAE	73	47,876.4	9.81%
Saudi Arabia	64	39,296.0	8.05%
Indonesia	216	19,924.1	4.08%
Qatar	19	19,245.6	3.94%
Bahrain	273	13,918.5	2.85%
Pakistan	57	6,348.9	1.30%
Turkey	9	5,469.7	1.12%
Brunei	95	4,980.7	1.02%
Kuwait	22	2,992.4	0.61%
Singapore	9	984.2	0.20%
United States	3	765.7	0.16%
United Kingdom	5	279.1	0.06%
China	3	274.7	0.06%
Yemen	2	251.5	0.05%
Sudan	3	220.9	0.05%
Germany	1	190.9	0.04%
Gambia	242	149.2	0.03%
Iran	4	132.8	0.03%
Jordan	1	120.3	0.02%
Japan	1	100.0	0.02%
Kazakhstan	1	73.3	0.02%
France	1	0.7	0.00%
Total	**3,594**	**488,172.5**	**100%**

Governments remain the most active issuers across the history of the global Sukuk market, with Malaysia's government leading. Sovereigns have issued a total of $280 billion since 1996. During the period 2010-2014, 72% of global Sukuk issuance or $248 billion came from governments, 18% from quasi government bodies ($34.1

billion), while only 10% or $64 billion were issued by corporates (chart 2).

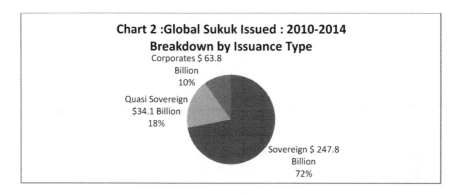

malaysia had a total of $325 billion Sukuk issued, with 67% sovereign, 13% quasi government bodies and 20% corporates. GCC corporates are far more active in the Sukuk market than their sovereigns but the total amount of both GCC sovereigns and quasi sovereigns marginally exceeds corporate issuance. A total of $123 billion GCC Sukuk were issued from 1996 to 2013, made up of 49% corporates, 20% quasi and 31% sovereign. Financial services came next after government institutions accounting for 12.7% of the value of aggregate Sukuk issued during the period 1996 till 2013, followed by power and utilities (6.8%), and real estate (5%).

Sukuk rating is important especially for corporates who do not enjoy government support and depend solely on their own performance. Around 45% of global Sukuk issued in 2012-2014 were rated. There were Sukuk issues for unrated corporates or those with sub-investment grade, nevertheless, these accounted for less than 30% of the total and provided a higher risk adjusted premium to investors looking for yield compared to the investment grade Sukuk.

Several western companies have issued Sukuk, including HSBC, Goldman Sachs, General Electric, and Tesco's Malaysian arm among others. All of them went through the long expensive process of dealing with Muslim scholars, lawyers and bankers to issue Sukuk at a time when issuing conventional bonds have never been easier or cheaper. The reason is to tap an alternative funding source for diversification and yield purposes.

As most Sukuk are traded over the counter, the need for listed Sukuk has been neglected despite its significance for transparency. Only around 6% of global Sukuk issued were listed in the last couple of years ($16.57 billion in 2013 and $21.4 billion in 2012). 32 out of 520 (6.15%) were listed in 2013, a slightly higher proportion than the 41 out of 672 (6.1%) in 2012. London Stock Exchange, Nasdaq Dubai, Saudi Arabia's Tadawul and Bursa Malaysia are the top stock exchanges holding most of these listed Sukuk. By 2014, London Stock Exchange was the home to 13 international Sukuk with a total value of $19 billion, while Nasdaq Dubai listed 22 Sukuk with a value of $20 billion.

Sukuk issues tend to have maturities no longer than five to seven years. However, on April 2014, the government of Dubai issued a 15-year Sukuk worth $750 million priced at 5% in an effort to build a longer-term yield curve. Some 61% of investors in the Sukuk, which has a common sale and leaseback structure known as Ijara, came from the Middle East, 17% from Britain, 10% from the rest of Europe and the balance from Asia and the US. The new issue, listed on Nasdaq Dubai, is traded and settled through Clearstream and Euroclear.

On average the cost of Sukuk issuance comprises around 1% of the total size of the issue. This is slightly higher than the corresponding cost of issuing conventional bonds. Liquidity and tradability derive the price gap between Sukuk and bonds, due mainly to the relatively smaller size of the global Sukuk market compared to the bond market. In addition, there is only $1.3 billion of shorter term Sukuk for treasuries of Islamic Financial Institutions to draw upon when investing their short-term surpluses.

Despite their higher issuing cost relative to bonds, Sukuk have benefited from specialist investors who would only consider sharia compliant product, as well as, other global investors seeking diversification and attractive yields. A survey conducted by Thomson Reuters in September 2013 found that the majority of corporates would still issue Sukuk even if the yield was 50 basis points higher than a conventional bond, while 55% of buyers would still opt for Sukuk as an asset class regardless of the yield.

4.5 Asset Backed Vis-à-Vis Asset Based Sukuk

Most investors prefer Sukuk backed by physical assets which are secured and give investors recourse to both the assets and the obligor's guarantee, compared to asset based Sukuk which are normally non-tradable, and difficult to liquidate in case of default with recourse only to the obligor's credit quality.

When Sukuk were first developed, the requirement was to have 100% tangible assets to provide full asset backing to investors. In asset-backed securities, the Sukuk holders enjoy the full backing of the underlying assets, as there is true sale and legal transfer of the ownership of the assets to Sukuk holders. The holders of Sukuk thus enjoy the guarantee of having recourse to the assets to cover their capital in the event the borrower becomes insolvent or faces difficulties in meeting payments.

However, corporates and governments faced challenges in finding the suitable assets for the structuring of such Sukuk. Either the assets were not available, or were not sufficient, or were already encumbered, or such sale of assets would be subject to transfer taxes. On the part of governments, especially in countries of the Gulf Cooperation Council (GCC), the law does not allow for the sale of public assets such as land and property to foreigners, which made the structuring of asset-backed sovereign Sukuk difficult.

Malaysia then issued in 2002 an asset based Sukuk Al-Ijara, which bore no true sale of the underlying assets to Sukuk holders, and instead assets were leased for a specific period and for an agreed amount of rental payments. In the event of default, Sukuk holders would have recourse to the Federation of Malaysia the (borrower/ obligor) rather than to the underlying assets of the Sukuk. From this first issuance of asset-based Sukuk, the structure has been widely used across the world. While asset-based Sukuk still require physical assets which are sharia-compliant to be leased in support of the Sukuk however, for those issuers who do not have sufficient physical assets, they were allowed to draw on sharia-compliant receivables, as long as, the minimum proportion of physical assets in the mixed portfolio were 30%.

Later on, asset-light Sukuk structures that do not require any physical assets at the time of issuance were introduced. These Sukuk were based on the concept of Mudaraba (profit sharing) or Musharaka (profit and loss sharing) agreements between the issuers and holders of Sukuk. Overtime, Sukuk became certificates that entitle the holder to a claim to an asset and/or to its cash flow. The asset-light Sukuk were strongly criticized by sharia scholars because i) Sukuk holders do not have real ownership interest in the underlying assets, or ii) the regular distributions to Sukuk holders (rent or profits) were not based on the actual performance of the underlying assets, and iii) guarantee of the return upon maturity of the principle amount to Sukuk holders at its par or nominal value, regardless of their market value on that day.

In recent years, the market has slowly been moving towards the Sukuk Wakala structure. The borrower (obligor) is appointed as agent (Wakil) to invest and mange the Sukuk proceeds, on behalf of the Sukuk holders. The Sukuk relies on a blended structure of tangible assets (sharia-compliant shares) and Murabaha receivables. The structure had the added advantage of allowing issuance above the value of available physical assets.

Based on 2002 to 2014 figures, which depict the trend of Sukuk issuance using various underlying sharia contracts, the global Sukuk market was dominated by Murabaha and Ijara structures. These mimicked conventional bonds with fixed periodic rental payments. Murabaha is a structure whereby a financial institution agrees to purchase an asset for a client provided that the client commits to purchase it back from the financial institution at an agreed mark up. Issues based on the Musharaka contract appear to have again recovered in 2012, reaching $15.37 billion, compared to Ijara Sukuk ($21.4 billion) and Murabaha Sukuk ($69.2 billion). Wakala Sukuk has also shown a steady growth since 2009 reaching $9 billion in 2014.

The implementation of new regulatory requirements, particularly Basel III, and the lack of high-quality liquid assets in the Islamic finance industry might increase sovereign and central bank's issuances and provide the Islamic finance industry with much-needed instruments to manage liquidity.

Central banks are looking at the experience of Bank Negara, the central bank of Malaysia, which is the established leader in Sukuk issuance. Total Sukuk issuance from central banks reached $50.2 billion in 2014, or 43.1% of all issuance, with Malaysia alone accounting for 92.1% of that at year-end 2014, followed by the Central Bank of Bahrain at 3.7%.

4.6 Developing the Local Project Finance Sukuk Market

With banks becoming less interested and/or willing to provide long-term funding, the debt capital market is seen as a potential alternative to finance infrastructural projects. Furthermore, because Islamic finance particularly Sukuk, are based on real assets, they are more suited to use in project finance structures. Malaysia has already used Sukuk structures to fund infrastructural development, showing that the potential is there.

The project finance Sukuk issued by SATORP, a joint venture refinery company owned by Aramco (62.5%) and Total (37.5%), promises a lot for the local currency and project finance Sukuk market in the region. SATORP's SR3.75 billion ($1 billion) Sukuk issued in November 2011 to finance part of the new refinery is notable for its long tenure of 14 years and its Saudi riyal denomination. Although one issue does not amount to a trend, however the sheer size of the potential pipeline will encourage participants to diversify funding requirements drawing increasingly more on Sukuk.

Saudi Arabia's General Authority for Civil Aviation, guaranteed by the Saudi Government, issued a massive 15.2 billion Saudi riyal ($4.05 billion) Sukuk in October 2013. The Saudi government has already indicated that a Sukuk would form part of the financing for the new airport in Jeddah, as well as, other infrastructural projects in electricity, water and natural gas. The Kingdom is planning to spend SR 1 trillion ($267 billion) on infrastructural projects during 2014-2017. Dubai's preparations for the 2020 World Expo and Qatar's plans for the 2022 FIFA World Cup are all likely to boost Sukuk issuance either directly by the sovereign or by related project finance entities. Oman, who has not been a major issuer, has also indicated that it will use Sukuk to fund infrastructural projects in the next few years. Going forward, government spending in countries like Egypt, Morocco, Tunisia, Libya and Jordan are likely to be partially funded through Sukuk.

4.7 The International Sukuk market

In 2002, the Malaysian government issued the first rated international Sukuk. The issuance of international Sukuk reached $24.7 billion in 2007 before dropping to $8.2 billion in 2008. However, issuance picked up speed in the following years with the cumulative new issuance of international Sukuk reaching $103 billion during the period 2009-2013. The GCC region accounted for 65% of the total, followed by Indonesia, Malaysia and Turkey.

The Sukuk market is still dominated by domestic issues, which represent 84% of the total market, with international Sukuk comprising only 16%. Cross-border Sukuk is another consideration. National Bank of Abu Dhabi completed two deals denominated in Malaysian ringgit in 2010 that totaled an equivalent of $325 million. The ringgit has so far been the dominant currency of the international Sukuk market accounting for 59.2% of the total, followed by the US dollar with 23.7% and with the Gulf currencies making the balance.

According to Thomson Reuter's 2014 Sukuk survey, around 50.6% of investors prefer to invest in international Sukuk, while 60% of lead arrangers believe that international Sukuk will be the most expected type of issuance in the coming years.

From the perspective of the global investor, there are two main issues impeding demand of international Sukuk. First, there is the issue of enforceability from a common law and sharia perspective. The second issue relates to the underlying assets that make Sukuk unique. As either asset-backed or asset-based securities, Sukuk are said to represent ownership. However, opaque reporting of underlying assets and often undisclosed or ill-defined ownership structures create challenges for international investors performing their required due diligence. This issue is evident with even a cursory examination of the information outlined in Sukuk prospectuses. Both these issues, which are somewhat interrelated, remain hotly debated among many stakeholders in the Islamic finance industry.

To highlight the issues pertaining to enforceability of sharia in different jurisdiction, consider a typical Sukuk issue from the Saudi Electricity Company (SEC). The SEC Sukuk issuance is a securitization of assets located in Saudi Arabia, a sharia-incorporated authority. In this case the asset originator is located in the same jurisdiction, while the special purpose vehicle (SPV), the Sukuk issuer is located in the Cayman Islands, a secular jurisdiction that allows for the choice of the applicable law for financial transactions.

The emergence of new sovereign issuers of international Sukuk, such as Britain, Luxembourg and Hong Kong, will broaden the market and help to ease a shortage of top rated paper, much sought after by Islamic financial institutions. The UK issued its first sovereign Sukuk valued at 200 million pounds ($330 million) in June 2014, it was followed by Hong Kong, Turkey, South Africa, Senegal and Luxembourg. Hopefully, other sovereign issuers who want to attract funds from the Gulf and Southeast Asia would follow suit. A silver lining of lower oil prices in 2015 is that there will be more sovereign Sukuk issuance to finance budgetary deficits.

4.8 Liquidity of the Sukuk Market

The small size of the Sukuk market compared to the conventional bond market, shortage of trading mechanisms and absence of active international players are the main reasons behind the limited liquidity and tradability in the secondary markets of Sukuk. There is also limited amount of short-term Sukuk for treasuries to invest their excess liquidity. Investors tend to hold Sukuk issues till maturity because they may not be able to purchase another Sukuk if they sell the one they possess. Sukuk are primarily held by Islamic banks, which are generally long-term hold-to-maturity players. Another factor inhibiting liquidity from the demand side is non-inclusion of regional Sukuk issues in any of the emerging market bond indices such as JP Morgan's EMBI Global Index. This restricts global bond funds/asset managers using such indices as benchmarks from allocating a portion of the assets under management to Sukuk issues.

It is noticeable that in all international and big Sukuk issuances, conventional banks take the role of lead arrangers and book runners of Sukuk while Islamic banks provide support to the issuance through distribution in their respective domestic markets. A lack of global international Islamic banks and the absence of dedicated traders providing bid/ask prices on a continuous basis is another constraint to deeper secondary Sukuk markets.

The Malaysia based International Islamic Liquidity Management Corp (IILM) owned by a consortium of central banks for Asia, the Middle East and Africa including the Jeddah based Islamic Development Bank was established in 2013 to help Islamic banks to manage their short-term funding needs by providing short-term liquid, investment grade sharia- compliant financial instruments. The IILM expanded on January 20, 2014 its regular auction of Islamic short-term Sukuk program by $370 million to $860 million, and introduced a $400 million of six months Sukuk in August 2014. The auctions of three months and six months Sukuk is conducted on a regular basis, with the aim of raising the target to $2 billion by the end of 2015 from its current level of $1.35 billion. The IILM also expanded the number of primary dealers handling the short-term Sukuk to nine from seven.

Growth in the size of the Sukuk market Vis-à-Vis the conventional bond market will greatly enhance liquidity in the secondary market for Sukuk. The following developments will also provide depth to the Sukuk market:

a.   While the GCC region will continue to be the main driver of growth in the Sukuk market, however going forward, we need to see a larger proportion of Sukuk in the gross new issuance of debt (bonds and Sukuk) coming from the region. Current proportion of 20% for Sukuk is low, to say the least. Sovereign issuers can take a lead by raising a higher portion of their debt funding through Sukuk, including shorter-term maturities to come up with a yield curve. Similarly, corporate issuers using both conventional and sharia-compliant financing can shift the balance in favor of Sukuk issues.

b. Higher pace of international Sukuk issuance is expected from markets such as Turkey, Indonesia, Malaysia and several European countries. For example, Turkey's conventional banks, which are regular issuers of debt, are currently not allowed to issue Sukuk. Change in the regulation by the Turkish central bank, can open doors for new Sukuk issues by local banks.

c. Evolution and acceptance of Sukuk financing across the capital structure will provide depth to the market. The launch in 2012 of the world first perpetual hybrid Sukuk by Abu Dhabi Islamic Bank in the UAE, which was eligible for treatment as Tier 1 equity (Basel III compliant Sukuk), was replicated by Dubai Islamic bank (DIB) in 2014, who issued $1 billion perpetual capital boosting Sukuk at 6.75%. Saudi Arabia's National Commercial Bank issued a SR5 billion ($1.3 billion) Sukuk in February 2014. By end of 2014, a total of eight Basel 3 compliant Sukuk have been issued raising close to $5 billion. Other Islamic banks in the region are expected to use the same structure to raise Tier 1 capital. Corporates are also increasingly looking at such perpetual Sukuk structures to raise equity capital.

d. Political stability of the Middle East and strong economic fundamentals are of prime significance, as these will affect the credit rating of Sukuk's issuers. Lower oil prices and rising need for budgetary expenditures may see several sovereign Sukuk coming to the market in 2015-2016.

4.9 The Way Forward

For Islamic finance to go mainstream, the focus needs to be on: (a) increasing access to finance and financial inclusion, (b) integrating Islamic finance instruments into public finance, (c) developing

Islamic finance markets and (d) building institutions and overcoming legal and regulatory hurdles. The MENA region has the lowest global account penetration rate and the least use of accounts to receive payments. According to the World Bank's Global Financial Inclusion database, 51% of adults globally report having an account at a formal financial institution. In the Organization of Islamic Countries (OIC), however, this rate is as low as 28% compared to 47% in other developing countries and 91% in developed countries. When it comes to credit, 33% of adults in OIC countries reported family or friends as one of their most important sources for new loans in 2014. Home construction and purchase form the main reason for borrowing. The signal is for OIC banks to focus on access to finance, housing finance and developing an Islamic finance mortgage backed Sukuk market.

Backed by strong demand, annual Sukuk issuance worldwide is expected to surge reaching $240 billion in 2018, more than double the 2014's level of $116 billion. The majority of Sukuk will come from asset-based structures in which investors rely on the issuer's ability to generate profits with these assets, as well as, direct support features like the credit strength of the issuer and the repurchase agreement.

Increasingly, more corporates will be issuing Sukuk. Islamic Gulf banks in particular may want to tap the market as tougher regulatory capital standards kick in (Sukuk hybrids can count towards capital). The UK made an inaugural Sukuk issue in June 2014, with the ambition to host a hub for Islamic finance in the non-Muslim world. Other sovereign issuers followed with their own Sukuk, opening the doors for corporates from those countries to follow suit.

With increasing sharia concerns raised about Sukuk structures, the key question to be asked is: How should the global Sukuk market move forward? Should all Sukuk structures, regardless of their underlying sharia contracts, maintain their original idea of being an alternative to conventional bonds, and thus become a fixed income instrument? Or, should Sukuk truly behave according to their specific underlying sharia contracts? As such, should all equity- based Sukuk move from the debt-like instrument to pure equity structures similar to stocks, where sharing of profit and loss is their essence? The answer to these questions lies with the ability of financial institutions to come up with innovative structures that will help make Sukuk an accessible and an acceptable financial instrument to use and invest in.

The lack of a centralized, global regulator in Islamic finance has so far been a double-edged sword. On the positive side it means financial institutions have a certain freedom in selling products as Sharia compliant which has helped the industry prosper. On the other hand, those investing for religious/ethical reasons may be misled in thinking some products are totally in line with the spirit of the Sharia, while in fact they are not. There is a risk of an inconsistent application of the principals of Islamic finance, which may result in greater confusion and ultimately, the loss of faith in these principals.

This had led to calls for greater international standardization, i.e. the creation by national regulators of Islamic finance a centralized global entity as the Islamic Financial Services Board, which issues both religious and prudential guidance, playing the same role as the Basel Committee does for conventional banks.

An independent legal body should oversee the way in which Islamic Financial Institutions follow sharia principles. Establishing such a body would involve challenges but it could take its cues from the conventional financial auditing profession. Accounting scandals at companies such as Enron have prompted regulators in some countries to require rotation of companies' auditors after a certain period of time. Companies have also been encouraged to use separate firms for their audit and advisory work. By contrast, appointments of scholars to sharia boards in the Gulf are often considered long-term or even permanent, and the scholars become involved in the design and sometimes even the marketing of Islamic financial products.

This is beginning to change, however, Oman introduced term limits for sharia scholars as part of an extensive Islamic banking rule book introduced in December 2012. Its rules require scholars to be appointed for three-year terms and serve a maximum of two consecutive terms, effectively requiring banks to hire new scholars periodically. Further progress would require input from industry bodies, such as Islamic Financial Services Board (IFSB), a top governing body for the industry that will enhance confidence of stakeholders and clients in the soundness of transactions from a sharia perspective.

However, governing bodies such as the IFSB have focused on prudential rules such as liquidity and stress testing of Islamic banks, rather than addressing the role of sharia scholars. The Bahrain-based Accounting and Auditing Organization for Islamic Financial Institutions (AAOIFI), a body that gathers the industry's most prominent scholars, has focused on guidance of financial instruments such as Sukuk. AAOIFI's standards do recognize that lengthy scholar appointments could lead to a close relationship, which could be perceived to be a threat to independence and objectivity, but it does not prescribe term limits. It recommends that institutions rotate at least one sharia board member every five years, but such guidelines are not enforceable in most countries and don't address the broader self-auditing issue.

CHAPTER 5

Mutual Funds: Giving Added Depth to the Region's Financial Markets

5.1 Introduction: Mutual Funds and ETFs

Mutual funds pool the financial resources of individuals and companies and invest those resources in (diversified) portfolios of assets. The range of assets covered by mutual funds (from property and stocks to bonds and Sukuk) provides an easy way for asset managers to give their clients exposure to different markets. Open-end mutual funds (the majority of mutual funds) sell new shares to investors and redeem outstanding shares on demand at their fair market values. They provide opportunities for small investors to invest in a liquid and diversified portfolio of financial securities. Thus, mutual funds can be viewed both as financial institutions and as a type of security investment. For small investors, mutual funds are also able to enjoy economies of scale by incurring lower transaction costs and commissions.

The first mutual fund was established in the USA in 1924. The industry grew very slowly at first, so that by 1970 there were 360 funds worldwide holding about $50 billion in assets. Since then, the number of funds and the asset size of the industry have increased dramatically. This growth is attributed to the advent of money market mutual funds in 1972 and to an explosion of special-purpose equity, bond, emerging market, and derivative funds. The tremendous increase in the market value of financial assets such as equities and the relatively low transaction cost that mutual funds provide to investors (particularly small investors) have caused the mutual fund industry to boom.

A growing number of the long-term mutual funds (approximately 25%) are index funds in which fund managers buy securities in proportions similar to those included in a specified major stock index (such as the S&P 500 Index). That is, index funds are designed to match the performance of a stock index. Because little research or aggressive management is necessary for index funds, management fees are lower and returns are often higher than more actively managed funds.

The difference in returns between actively managed funds and passively managed index funds can be explained as follows: For example, during the 1990s, the S&P 500 had an annualized return of 17.3%, while the average actively managed mutual funds investing in the US stock market had an annualized return of 13.9%. The 3.4% difference is explained first by the fact that during the 1990s the S&P 500 (an index consisting of the 500 largest companies in America) produced returns that were better than the rest of the market. Further, the average amount of expenses that an actively managed fund charges its shareholders every year is approximately 1.4%, compared to S&P 500 index fund of 0.19%. Also, actively managed funds turn over their holdings rapidly. This turnover occurs at an average rate as high as 85% per year. The transaction costs involved in buying and selling so many shares every year result in an additional 2% of return disappearing every year.

Exchange-traded funds (ETFs) are long-term mutual funds that are also designed to replicate a particular stock market index. However, unlike index funds, ETFs are traded on a stock exchange at prices that are determined by the market. Assets invested in ETFs totaled $2,500 billion at the end of 2014, up from $423 billion at the end of 2006. ETFs include funds such as SPDRs (replicating S&P 500 index) and Vanguard's Large-Cap VIPERS funds.

Like index funds, the share price of an ETF changes over time in response to a change in the stock prices underlying a stock index.

Further, since both ETFs and index funds are intended to track a specific index, management of the funds is relatively simple and management fees are lower than those of actively managed mutual funds (around 0.25% a year compared with 1%-2% charged by most mutual funds). Unlike index funds, however, ETFs can be traded during the day, they can be purchased on margin, and they can be sold short by an investor who expects a drop in the underlying index value. Because ETFs behave like stocks, investors are subject to capital gains taxes only when they sell their shares. Thus, ETF investors can defer capital gains for as long as they hold the ETF.

Price Waterhouse Coopers projected global assets under management (AUM) to reach $101.7 trillion at the end of 2020, compared to $65 trillion at the end of 2014, constituting a compounded annual growth rate of 6% between 2014 and 2020. It forecasts AUM in North America at $49.4 trillion at the end of 2020, with a compounded annual growth of 5.1% during the 2014-20 period, those in Europe at $27.9 trillion (+4.4%), in Asia-Pacific at $16.2 trillion (+9.8%), in Latin America at $6.7 trillion (+12.5%) and AUM in the Middle East & Africa at $1.5 trillion (+11.9%). The distribution of global assets under management by region for 2014 is given in chart 1.

Source: *Price Waterhouse Coopers, 2015.*

5.2 Calculation of Net Asset Value of Mutual Funds

The return for the investor from investing in mutual fund shares reflects three aspects of the underlying portfolio of mutual fund assets. First, the portfolio earns income and dividends on those assets. Second, capital gains occur when the mutual fund sells an asset at prices higher than the original purchase price of the asset. Third, capital appreciation in the underlying values of its existing assets adds to the value of mutual fund units. With respect to capital appreciation, mutual fund assets are normally marked to market daily. This means that the managers of the fund calculate the current value of each mutual fund unit by computing the daily market value of the fund's total asset portfolio and then dividing this amount by the number of mutual fund units outstanding. The resulting value is called the net asset value (NAV) of the fund. This is the price that investors obtain when they sell units or buy new ones in the fund that day.

Mutual funds are open end in that the number of units outstanding fluctuates daily with the amount of unit redemptions and new purchases. With open-end funds, investors buy and sell units from and to the mutual fund company. Thus, the demand for units determines the number of units outstanding, and the market value of the underlying securities held in the mutual fund divided by the number of shareholders outstanding determines the NAV of units.

As an example, suppose a mutual fund contains 200 shares of company X, 300 shares of company Y and 500 shares of company Z. The mutual fund has 1500 units held by investors. If today's share prices of X, Y, and Z are $30, $50 and $80 respectively then today's Net Asset Value (NAV) of the fund is calculated as

$$NAV = \frac{\text{Total Market Value of assets under management}}{\text{Number of Mutual funds Units outstanding}}$$

$$NAV = \frac{(200 \times \$30) + (300 \times \$50) + (500 \times \$80)}{1500} = \$40.6$$

If tomorrow X's shares increase to $35, Y's shares decrease to $45 and Z's shares increase to $85, and suppose that 100 new units in the fund were sold to additional investors at the NAV of $40.6. This means the manager has an additional $4060 funds to invest and the fund has now 1600 units held by investors. Suppose that the fund manager decides to use these additional funds to buy Y's shares whose price has dropped to $45. At today's market price the manager could buy 90 additional shares of Y ($4060/$45). The Fund's new portfolio will now have: 200 shares of X, 390 shares of Y and 500 shares of Z. The new NAV of the Fund will be

$$NAV = \frac{(200 \times \$35) + (390 \times \$45) + (500 \times \$85)}{1500 + 100} = \frac{67,050}{1600} = \$41.9$$

Note that the fund's NAV changed ($41.9 versus $40.6) due to both capital appreciation and size of the fund.

The cost of mutual fund investing to the shareholder includes both the one-time sales or placement fee and any annual fees charged. Suppose an individual invests $10,000 in a mutual fund. The placement fee entails an up-front commission charge of 4% of the amount invested and is deducted from the original funds invested. Thus, the individual's actual investment, after the placement fee is deducted, is:

$10,000 (1 - .04) = $9,600

In addition, annual fund operating and management expenses are 0.85%. The annual fees are charged on the average net asset value invested in the fund and are recorded at the end of each year. Assuming that investments in the fund return 5% each year paid on the last day of the year. If the investor reinvests the annual returns paid on the investment, after one year the operating fees deducted and the value of the investment are:

Annual operating expenses = average net asset value x annual operating expenses
= [$9,600 + $9,600(1.05)]/2 x .0085 = $83.640

Value of investment at end of year1 = $9,600(1.05) - $83.640 = $9,996.360
This investor's return on the mutual fund investment after one year is:
($9,996.360 - $10,000)/$10,000 = -0.04%

In year 2, the investor's fees deducted and investment value at the end of the year are:

Annual operating expenses = [$9,996.360 + $9,996.360(1.05)]/2 x .0085 = $87.093

Value of investment at end of year 2 = $9,996.360(1.05) - $87.093 = $10,409.085

After 2 years the investor has paid a total of $400 in placement fees and $170.733 in operating expenses, and he has made $409.085 above the original $10,000 investment. The investor' annual return on the mutual fund is therefore 2.02%.

5.3 What to Look for When Choosing a Mutual Fund

The criteria that mutual fund managers use to select their assets vary widely according to the individual manager. So when choosing a fund, the investor should look closely at the manager's investment style to make sure it fits his risk-reward profile. Investment style is very important because of the way it works. Both risk and return are connected to style. According to current practice portfolio theory, you can optimize a blend of styles for diversification and for balancing reward and risk. The six common investment strategies among fund managers include: Top-down investing, Bottom-up investing, Fundamental analysis, Technical analysis, Contrarian investing and Dividend investing.

Top-down investing strategies involve choosing assets based on a big theme. For example, if a fund manager anticipates that the economy will grow sharply, he might buy stocks across the board, or the manager might choose to buy stocks in particular economic sector that are likely to experience high growth. If the manager expects the economy to slump, it may spur them to sell stocks (short the market) or purchase shares in defensive industries.

The great advantage of top-down is that you are looking at the forest rather than the trees. That makes screening for stocks or other investments easier. Of course, managers might be wrong on their big idea, and even if they're right, that doesn't guarantee they will always succeed in choosing the right investments.

Bottom-up managers choose stocks based on the strength of an individual company, regardless of what is happening in the economy as a whole or the sector in which that company lies. A bottom-up manager benefits from thorough research on an individual company, but a market plunge often pulls even the strongest investments down.

Fundamental analysis involves evaluating all the factors that affect an investment's performance. For a specific stock, it would mean looking at all of the company's financial information to come up with an assessment of whether the company is properly valued, overvalued or undervalued. It may also entail meeting with company executives, employees, suppliers, customers and competitors.

Technical analysis involves choosing assets based on prior trading patterns. You are looking at the trend of an investment's price. If the price is on an up cycle you buy, if a correction cycle is in place it is an indication to sell.

Most managers emphasize fundamental analysis, because they want to understand what will drive growth. Investors expect the stock price to rise if a company is showing higher profits. Some managers use both fundamental and technical analysis. If a stock has good fundamentals, it should be a good buy on the medium to long term. Technical analysis is more useful for intraday trading or for short cycles.

Contrarian managers choose assets that are out of favor. They determine the market's consensus about a company or sector and then go against it. The contrarian style is generally aligned with a value-investing strategy, which means buying assets that are undervalued by some statistical measure (P/E, price to book, dividend yield). The risk with this strategy is that it goes against the consensus. This normally results in wrong bets and losses for a contrarian manager, except in very few cases where it works. These include funds that buy stocks with a strong record of earnings offering investors a regular pay out. Even if the price goes down, there is still some income being generated. Such funds suits investors who are retired and live on interest earned and dividends distributed.

5.4 Size and Structure of Mutual Funds in the MENA Region

The mutual funds industry in the MENA region is still in its early stages of development with assets under management (AUM) as a percentage of the region's GDP accounting for a small 2%, compared to 8% in India, 48% in Brazil and 78% in the USA (chart 2). AUM of mutual funds in the region as a percentage of bank deposits is also small at 4%, compared to 15% in India, 103% in Brazil and 143% in the USA. This points to a lack of mutual fund penetration. The use of mutual funds as an investment vehicle has a long way to go in most, if not all, countries of the region.

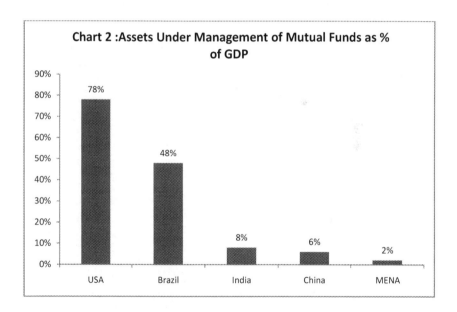

Chart 2 :Assets Under Management of Mutual Funds as % of GDP

With global assets under management in 2014 of $65 trillion, 50% of which in North America, the MENA region accounted for less than 0.1% of world total. There were around 782 mutual funds investing in the region's capital markets in 2014 including all funds that have the MENA region or one of its constituent countries as their geographical focus, irrespective where these funds are domiciled. Saudi Arabia had the highest AUM in the region of close to $22 billion, accounting for

35.3% of total AUM in the region and comprising both conventional as well as Islamic funds (table 1). It was followed by Morocco with AUM of $13.9 billion accounting for 22.6% and Egypt with $11.1 billion (18.1% share).

Table 1: **Mutual Funds in the MENA Region: Number of Funds and Asset Under Management**

Geographical Focus of the Fund	Conventional Funds		Islamic Funds		Total		Average	2014	
	No. of Funds	AUM ($mn)	No. of Funds	AUM ($mn)	No. of Funds	AUM ($mn)	Funds Size (mn)	GDP ($bn)	AUM As % of GDP
Saudi Arabia	93	2,529	83	19,241	122	21,769	178	727	3%
Morocco	174	13,929	2	15	176	13,943	79	98	14%
Egypt	75	11,043	11	102	86	11,145	130	257	4%
Kuwait	22	2,981	21	1,143	43	4,115	96	173	2%
Tunisia	108	3,070	4	4	112	3,074	27	46	7%
GCC	32	1,639	43	1,196	75	2,835	38	NA	NA
MENA	81	1,853	28	647	109	2,499	23	NA	NA
Lebanon	12	815	0	-	12	815	68	41	2%
UAE	14	605	3	97	17	703	41	359	0%
Oman	6	401	0	-	6	401	67	76	1%
Qatar	9	316	4	49	13	365	28	183	0%
Iraq	7	44	0	-	7	44	6	212	0%
Jordan	3	20	0	-	3	20	7	31	0%
Bahrain	1	1	0	-	1	7	7	27	0%
Total	637	39,246	199	22,485	782	61,735	795	2,230	34%

Breaking down MENA's fund assets by product, money market funds come first with 31%, followed by trade finance and leasing funds at 27%, equities at 23%, fixed income funds (bonds and Sukuk funds) at 15% and specialized sector specific funds for the remaining 4% (chart 3). In Egypt and Morocco, money market funds account for a high of 93% and 45% of total AUM respectively, while in Saudi Arabia, trade finance funds account for 70% of total assets under management.

Chart 3: Break Down of MENA
Assets Under Management by Product (%)

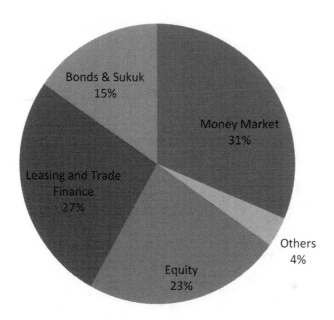

The breakdown of Global funds shows a slightly different distribution of AUM by product, with equity accounting for 41% of the total, followed by bonds and money market instruments with 22% and 19% respectively (chart 4).

Chart 4: Break Down of Global
Fund Assets Under Management by Product (%)

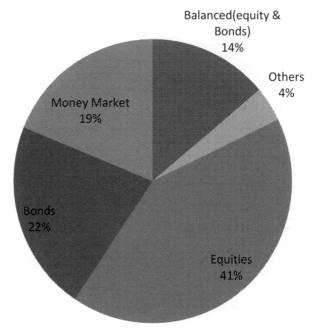

In terms of the number of funds by country, Morocco comes first with 176 funds, accounting for 22% of total number of funds in the region, followed by Saudi Arabia with 122 funds accounting for 15.6% of the total, and Tunisia with 112 funds accounting for 14.3%.

The MENA asset management market is concentrated among the top 20 asset managers (out of 175 managers) accounting for 75% of the total fund management sector. The National Commercial Bank (NCB Capital) of Saudi Arabia leads the list of the largest asset management companies in the region in 2014, with $15.7 billion in assets, followed by Investcorp ($11.4 billion), Abraj Group ($7.5 billion), Jadwa Investment of Saudi Arabia ($5.2 billion), Wafra ($5.1 billion), Riyadh Capital ($4.7 billion), Belton Asset Management ($4.5) and National Bank of Kuwait (NBK Capital) ($4.4 billion). (table 2).

Table 2: **Middle East's Top 20 Money Managers: 2014**

Rank	Firm	Location	Total Assets Under Management ($MN)
1	NBC Capital	Saudi Arabia	15,708
2	Investcorp Bank	Bahrain	11,420
3	Abraaj Group	UAE	7,500
4	Jadwa Investment	Saudi Arabia	5,187
5	Wafra International Investment Co.	Kuwait	5,122
6	Riyadh Capital	Saudi Arabia	4,757
7	Belfone Asset Management	Egypt	4,548
8	Watani Investment Co. (NBK Capital)	Kuwait	4,448
9	EFG-Hermes Holding SAE-Asset Management	Egypt	3,132
10	NBAD Asset Management Group (National Bank of Abu Dhabi)	UAE	2,962
11	Global Investment House	Kuwait	2,876
12	Emirates NBD Asset Management	UAE	2,559
13	Kuwait Financial Centre (Markaz)	Kuwait	1,887
14	First Investor	Qatar	1,240
15	EIIB-Rasmala Group	UAE	1,182
16	Swicorp	Saudi Arabia	1,029
17	Al Rayan Investment	Qatar	682
18	Ajeej Capital	Saudi Arabia	650
19	Kipco Asset Management Co.	Kuwait	324
20	Duet Mena	UAE	615

With the exception of Morocco, the fund management business in the Gulf countries is much more advanced than elsewhere in the region, with AUM in the six GCC countries put at $27 billion, spread among 75 funds. Equity funds account for the bulk of that with $11.3 billion in 46 funds followed by fixed income with $1.5 billion, money market ($477 million), and specialized funds ($149 million).

In general fund managers in the region tend to focus on the largest stocks in the market because they are the most liquid. This makes it very difficult to perform better than the benchmark, particularly after costs and fees are deducted.

5.5 SWOT Analysis of Mutual Funds In the Region

Strengths

- Establishment of regional financial centers/hubs.
- Steady progress in regulatory aspect.
- Ownership of distribution channels
- by commercial banks.
- Strong demand for professionally managed funds as investment vehicles.

Opportunities

- Inclusion of UAE and Qatar into MSCI Emerging Market Indices, and prospects of Saudi Arabia joining these indices.
- Broad scope for Islamic financial products (leasing and trade finance) and increased issuance of Sukuk.
- Underpenetrated markets (as percentage of funds to market capitalization) in comparison to Asian and Developed markets.
- Diversification of international portfolios with regional mandates (MENA).

Weaknesses

- Poor disclosures and weak corporate governance.
- Higher distribution costs as a result of single channel mode of distribution.
- Shortage of human resources with required technical skills.
- Lack of institutional participation/foreign investors.
- Non-availability of hedging products.
- Difficulty of valuing assets of Islamic mutual funds.

Threats

- Mounting of regional risk and social unrest/turmoil can influence investment climate.
- Lack of liquidity in the region's capital markets.
- Skewed sector representation in indices.
- Lack of unified regulations and constant amendments increases cost of compliance.
- Smaller fund sizes.
- Sustained low oil prices.

5.6 Products and Distribution of Funds

The mutual fund industry in the region does not provide much diversification in terms of products. The largest number of funds, estimated at 332 in 2014 provided exposure to the region's equity markets, either as conventional equity funds or Islamic funds that are restricted to sharia compliant stocks. Specialized funds came next at 179, followed by bonds and Sukuk funds (157), money market funds (82) and trade finance funds (32). There are more conventional funds in the region (583 funds) than Islamic funds (199 funds).

The specialized funds account for 4.1% of total AUM and they range from sector specific funds focused on say real estate, telecom, Banking and finance, to more specific funds such as those dedicated to IPOs, capital protection and balanced funds. These types of funds are expected to grow over the coming years and to attract diverse institutional and foreign investors.

Funds specializing in fixed income and Sukuk are gaining popularity, and Exchange Traded Funds (ETFs) have recently been introduced to the markets of the region. There are ten index funds with total AUM of $60 million, that track country and regional indices. For example, the Global GCC large cap fund, one of Global Investment House's flagship funds has outperformed its Benchmark in 2013, reporting a return of 35.2% compared to 22.6% by the S&P GCC index.

A few derivative instruments have been introduced to the market, with Kuwait Financial Center (Markaz) operating the Forsa Fund since 2004, which issues call options on Kuwaiti listed stocks. However, most markets of the region have shunned derivatives, which are seen to be in conflict with the basic principle of sharia.

Most of the mutual funds are domiciled in their respective domestic markets where local investors make up the bulk of participants in these funds. For example in 2014, there were 156 funds domiciled in Saudi Arabia, managing $23.1 billion in assets, followed by Morocco with 176 funds managing $13.9 billion. Outside the region, Jersey Island is the location where most of the MENA funds have been domiciled. To diversify the investor base and attract more foreign and institutional investors, we would expect managers to increasingly turn to other destinations, such as Luxembourg and Ireland for domiciliation of their funds.

Distribution of funds in the region is done either directly, purchasing fund units from the asset manager, targeting large investors (minimum subscription of $50,000), or indirectly through a third party usually commercial banks for retail distribution. Bank customers are often the target group to whom funds are sold. Several asset managers enjoy exclusive access to their parent bank distribution network, while others have signed agreements with banks to serve as their exclusive distributers. Third party distributers have their own infrastructure to carry out purchase and redemption orders.

The marketing and distribution of mutual funds are based on generally accepted principles of disclosure as specified in the fund's prospectus. However, the level of disclosure required by the regulatory authorities for funds targeting retail investors are higher than the disclosure requirements of funds targeting institutional investors.

As the mutual fund market in the region matures, multi-channel mode of distribution would take hold and the accompanying distribution cost would fall as had happened in the developed markets. Distribution costs for equity funds in the USA fell by 73% on the average between 1980 and 2001, while those of bond funds dropped by 60%.

5.7 Exchange Traded Funds

Exchange traded funds (ETFs) have been around since 1990, when the first ETF fund was launched in Canada. The original idea was to create portfolios of shares replicating a stock market index, such as S&P 500. Index tracking funds had been available to institutional investors since the 1970s. However, the difference between index funds and ETFs is that the later itself is traded on a stock market, so that investors can buy or sell it easily. ETFs allow small investors to own a diversified portfolio of stocks at a low cost. Most ETFs have expense ratio of less than 1%. While mutual fund redemptions can force fund managers to sell stocks, with ETFs, the underlying portfolio remains the same when an investor buys or sells ETF units. Unlike index funds, ETFs can be purchased on margin and can be sold short by an investor who expects a drop in the underlying index.

The global market for ETFs has doubled in size in just four years, reaching $2.6 trillion in 2014, with close to 3,867 ETFs listed on 50 exchanges worldwide. The US accounts for around 71% of the global ETF industry assets, followed by the EU (17.5%), Asia Pacific (4.1%), Japan (3.6%), Canada (2.5%) and Latin America (0.4%). Currently, only Saudi Arabia and the UAE have ETFs listed on their exchanges, three on Tadawul and one on Abu Dhabi Securities Exchange (ADX). ETF assets in the region remain small, not exceeding $30 million for the four ETFs.

ETFs domiciled in the region have struggled for a number of reasons. They are all equity ETFs with no fixed income diversification. They have small sizes and thus are not attractive to institutional investors. Other reasons could be the absence of independent custodian, administrator and market makers. The index provider for these ETFs is Tadawul and ADX, rather than the major international index providers. Besides, investors in the region in general still believe that the scope to generate "alpha", or selecting a portfolio that outperforms the market, is high which reduces the need for a passive (beta) investment strategy as the one generated by ETFs.

The first sharia compliant ETF in the region was introduced by HSBC in the second half of 2011. The HSBC Amanah Saudi 20 ETF aims to replicate the performance of the 20 Equity index made up of the top 20 sharia-compliant Saudi companies listed on Tadawul. The other two ETFs in Saudi Arabia are those of Falcom, one replicating the Saudi stock market and the other listed stocks of petrochemical companies in the Kingdom. Non-GCC residents are allowed to invest in the ETFs listed on Tadawul. The ETF listed on ADX follows the performance of 25 blue-chip companies listed in Dubai and Abu Dhabi.

5.8 Islamic Asset Management

Assets under management by Islamic Funds worldwide did not exceed $100 billion in 2014, a small number compared to total global assets under management in excess of $60 trillion. If the Islamic mutual funds were to tap just one per cent of the industry's world total, it would mean $600 billion, generating management fees of $6 billion, assuming net fees on AUM of 1%.

The size of most of the Islamic funds is relatively small, with more than half the existing funds having assets under management of less than $100 million. This in itself is a limiting factor for further growth as institutional investors favor the big and the already established players in the market.

Another constraint is the lack of diversification with 46% of Islamic assets under management being equity based. However, this is changing gradually. The Islamic fund management industry has seen growing interest from investors in products that mimic fixed income investment. As a result the market is witnessing several Sukuk funds being launched. There are many retail investors who cannot invest directly in Sukuk issues because of the size of the upfront investment and would be served better with a well-managed Sukuk fund.

The biggest limit to growth in the Islamic asset management industry comes from the lack of high quality Islamic assets. Sharia compliant funds are not allowed to invest in financial institutions (banks, insurance companies, etc.) that deal in interest based instruments. Also they are banned from investing in highly leveraged companies (those with debt to equity ratio in excess of 33 per cent), and in companies involved in the production and marketing of prohibited goods and services like alcohol, tobacco, lottery and gambling. Companies who have a lot of assets in the form of receivables or those who do not have real assets (internet based companies) are also not considered to be sharia compliant.

Distribution of sharia compliant mutual funds across borders is further complicated by the differences in interpretation of sharia laws between the different Islamic schools. Where there are major differences of interpretations between countries, different funds with their own sharia boards may be needed to meet investor requirements in these countries.

Standardization of sharia laws is necessary for the Islamic mutual fund industry to acquire cross border scale to continue to grow and flourish. Until that happens, funds will tend to be launched on a country-by-country basis to serve local market places. Currently, about 22% of the sharia compliant funds are domiciled in Malaysia and 18% in Saudi Arabia with the UAE following as a distant third.

Two of the critical challenges facing the Islamic mutual fund industry revolve around the costs of running the funds and the difficulty of valuing assets. The higher cost of sharia compliant funds relates partly to the setting up and financing of sharia boards, a cost that the conventional fund industry does not have to bear. The screening process can also be expensive and the lack of scale in many funds magnifies the effect of costs. Valuation of assets center on the fact that not all issues that the sharia fund invests in trade on secondary markets, particularly the Sukuk. In this case, it is hard to evaluate what represents true and fair value for the redemption of price units. However, as the average fund size increases and markets become deeper and more liquid, the impact of cost and valuation of assets would become less of an issue.

Despite the constraints and challenges, the Islamic mutual fund industry is projected to grow at double-digit rates reaching $700 billion by 2020. It is estimated that Muslims own $3.5 trillion of assets worldwide; implying less than 3% of Muslim wealth ($100 billion) is currently managed in a sharia compliant fashion.

5.9 Active Vis-à-Vis Passive Mutual Funds

Asset management in the region has so far been in the shadows of banking. Going forward, asset management will become more of a stand-alone activity with banks serving as distribution channels.

The burden of retirement provision in the region is increasingly falling on the individual. Outside the GCC countries, the social security or the state pension funds offer on retirement little more than a subsistence income, giving the asset management industry an opportunity to step in and fill the gap.

Sovereign wealth funds in the region have been accumulating immense amount of new wealth and would like to invest more of it in the region's bond and equity markets. This will give added depth to these markets, and facilitate the growth of asset management business. Also, the rising demand on sharia compliant products will give a big boost to the Islamic fund industry in the years ahead.

Individual managers have to make a series of choices. Do they emphasize their skill of managing portfolios ("alpha") or head down the passive ("beta") route through the introduction of more ETFs? Do they stick to traditional asset classes, such as real estate, equities and bonds, or branch out into alternative areas such as leasing, hedge funds and commodities? Do they stay small, aiming for boutique status and putting emphasis on performance, or do they aim big, covering as many areas as possible? Should they concentrate on the relationship with individual clients or draw on third parties for distributing their funds?

In fund management, size is not necessarily an advantage. Although size can bring an improvement in margins (managing $2 billion does not cost twice as much as managing $1 billion) and can give managers the marketing clout to build a brand name and attract large institutional investors, nevertheless, size can also be the enemy of investment performance. If a fund becomes too large targeting thinly trading markets, trading would move prices against the manager, or the fund starts to resemble the overall market.

MENA asset management industry manages close to $65 billion in mutual funds while the country of Kuwait alone has assets worth $64 billion in managed portfolios. The preference for managed portfolios can be gauged from the fact that they are highly customizable and tailored to meet individual investing needs. Personalized service offering and the ability to have a directional influence on these portfolios add to the allure of managed accounts. As markets mature, mutual fund assets may experience higher growth over managed portfolios/accounts and should be able to attract a sizeable portion of these assets.

Going forward the industry will increasingly be affected on the institutional side by the shift of investors towards passive investments such as ETFs. On the retail side, the traditional actively managed funds will continue to be the core of the industry, however, it will grow at a lower rate than funds following passive and alternative strategies.

The National Bank of Abu Dhabi (NBAD) has rebranded several of its equity funds moving its investment focus to a broader Middle East and North Africa (MENA) from a UAE emphasis. Other fund managers may follow suite. The expanded scope, diversification and geography of the rebranded regional funds will offer new opportunities to institutional and retail investors.

A new breed of regional fund managers will soon emerge, one with highly streamlined platforms, targeting solutions for the customer with a stronger and more trusted brand. These managers will not only cater to local and regional investors but also to international institutional investors. Asset management operates within a relatively low-tech infrastructure. By 2020, technology will have become mission critical to drive customer engagement. The emphasis will be on data mining for information on customers and potential clients, as well as, operational efficiency and regulatory and tax reporting. At the same time, cyber risk will have become one of the key factors to monitor and manage the industry, ranking alongside operational, market and performance risk.

The successful asset managers of 2020 will have already started to shape their responses to some or all of these game changers. Those that develop coherent strategies and act with integrity towards clients are likely to build the brands that will not only be successful in 2020 but also trusted.

CHAPTER 6

The Development of World Class Financial Centers In the Region

6.1 Introduction: Financial Centers and Stock Exchanges

Today's financial centers where big financial transactions are executed and a wide array of financial products are traded include not only long established places such as New York, London and Tokyo, but also a growing number of newer financial hubs in Asia, the Middle East and elsewhere. As Dubai has shown, following in Singapore's earlier footsteps, a determined government can build an international financial center from scratch.

Financial centers are increasingly dependent on their connections to one another. Technology, the mobility of capital and the spread of deregulation around the globe have created a vibrant and growing network. When one city is asleep, another is awake, so trading goes on round the clock. The number of transactions between financial centers has surged recently as investors have diversified across regions and asset types. Yet interconnectedness has a cost. In an era of greater volatility, the latest market news spreads from one continent to another in an instant, with knock-on effects on other assets such as real estate, commodities and others.

New York and London have firmly established themselves at the top of the list providing one stop shop for a full range of financial services. But even the biggest centers cannot afford to be complacent. New York, still number one in global financial terms by many measures has recently acknowledged the competition it faces from other centers. London has surged on a wave of new money and talent, but it has other advantages including its time zone. London's trading day starts as Tokyo's market closes and few hours before New York opens. The widespread use of English around the world gives London an edge over Frankfurt, Paris or Zurich. The legal system is also supportive with a world's recognized commercial law firmly in place, implemented by experienced judges.

The leading financial centers score well on a package of key criteria that global financial firms are looking for: availability of skilled people, ready access to capital, good infrastructure, attractive regulatory and tax environments and low levels of corruption. Location and the use of English, the language of global finance, are also important. Based on those measures, a survey by the Economist magazine published September 17, 2010 picked London, New York and Hong Kong as the worlds top three financial centers.

Although New York and London are pre-eminent, other big cities play important international roles of their own. Some have prospered as the financial capitals of big national markets (Tokyo and Sydney) or the gateways to emerging regions (Hong Kong, Singapore and Dubai). Others have found success in niches, such as Geneva (private banking), Zurich (insurance and reinsurance), Chicago (futures and options), Qatar (infrastructure finance) and Bahrain (Islamic finance).

Aside from the political and economic gains to the host countries, there are two wider benefits from having a range of financial centers around the world. One is the increase in overall liquidity as new countries and regions become integrated into the global financial system. The second is increased efficiency as competition between centers drives down the cost of trading and other financial transactions. New and developing financial centers are knocking down protectionist barriers and emulating the regulatory practices of the more established financial hubs.

The cities that dominate today's financial world are connected not only by mobile capital and people, but also by stock exchanges as well. Exchanges have traditionally been at the heart of important financial cities. They were established to service mainly national markets, but have changed fundamentally in recent years to become more global. A growing number of them are now publicly owned, which have forced them to operate more efficiently and compete more openly.

Stock exchanges are also teaming up across national borders. The first ever-transatlantic merger between exchanges took place in 2007, when the New York Stock Exchange bought Euronext, a pan-European exchange group. The London Stock Exchange merged with Borsa Italiana, Italy's main market. Deutsche Borse teamed up the International Securities Exchange in New York. The big exchanges in Western countries are linking up as well with counterparts farther east, (e.g. Nasdaq with Dubai International Financial Exchange (DIFX) to form Nasdaq Dubai).

The stock exchange industry worldwide has experienced a major change in the past two decades, whereby most large international exchanges now operate as private and in some cases listed companies. This transformation of exchanges has initiated an intensive debate on the role of stock exchanges in the regulation and oversight of listed companies. Until recently, this debate has had little echo in the MENA region, where most stock exchanges are government-owned and some are structured as mutually owned organizations. The interest in restructuring the ownership and the legal form of Arab exchanges has grown in recent years. Several Arab Stock Exchanges such as the Jordanian and the Egyptian exchanges are interested in exploring ownership transitions. The management of these exchanges considers that private ownership might afford them greater operational flexibility and ultimately, ability to be more competitive regionally and perhaps internationally.

Most stock exchanges in the region are not under extreme pressure as far as listing and trading are concerned. One possible source of competition for them is the London Stock Exchange. These are currently 33 companies from the MENA region listed on London's main market, 25 of which are dual listings. However, it would be difficult to make the case that Arab exchanges are in competition with foreign markets because so far only few Arab companies have opted to list abroad.

It is plausible to argue that this competition will increase in the longer term as more large Arab companies are tempted to list in London or New York, or even Hong Kong. It is also not clear if one or more Arab exchanges might become the "center of gravity" in the region. In principle, Tadawul, the most liquid Arab stock market, may be well positioned to do so. The Casablanca Stock Exchange has also made efforts to attract listings from the African continent, trying to position itself as a choice of listing venue for African Companies.

On the other hand, private sector ownership of exchanges might allow exchanges to deal with the political sensitivities surrounding consolidation that many observers see as a prerequisite for Arab capital markets to appear more prominently on the radar screen of large international investors. Large institutional investors and asset managers consider MENA markets too small and this is why they are not getting as much attention in their portfolios as Asian or Latin American markets. In this sense therefore, the potential ownership transitions of Arab exchanges from public to private sector hands might help promote consolidation among stock exchanges in the region.

6.2 Key Drivers for the Success of Financial Centers

There are four key drivers for the development of a world-class financial center: **a.** Proximity to strong economic activity, **b.** Robust legal and regulatory framework, **c.** Availability of talent, both domestic and multinational, and **d.** Quality of life that the center provides.

a. Proximity to Strong Economic Activity

Financial markets flourish when the economic activities they support are thriving. Historically, financial centers have prospered in or around strong economies experiencing ample growth opportunities generating demand for financial services. London, New York, Hong Kong and Singapore continue to benefit from rising activities in the economic regions they are supporting. A large share of global finance is generated in these hubs, and almost three quarters of the world's equity trading is undertaken through their stock exchanges. These centers thrive on supporting large conglomerates operating in their backyard, requiring such services as trade and project finance, raising of debt and equity, mergers and acquisitions, asset and wealth management, insurance and brokerage among others.

As the share of emerging markets in the global economy rises, their potential as financial markets grows as well. Besides, financial flows from the advanced to the emerging economies are expected to be lower than the levels seen in the past, suggesting that much of the financing needs in the coming years will be met by emerging financial markets. Many of those markets have laid the foundation for their own financial hubs, pursuing national, regional, or even global ambitions. The most important include Shanghai becoming China's leading financial center, Mumbai serving as India's financial hub, while Dubai has become the Middle East's premier financial center.

b. Robust Legal and Regulatory Framework

Having in place a regulatory framework that insures financial stability and promotes market efficiency and innovation will be another key driver for the development of financial centers. This includes revising laws to accommodate new financial products, training judges and lawyers to better understand financial services, facilitating greater use of arbitration, raising corporate governance standards and adopting internationally accepted regulatory practices.

One of the key consequences of the 2008-2009 financial crisis has been the lack of tolerance for unregulated products and markets. Financial centers that do not comply with international rules regarding corruption, money laundering, taxation and prudential standards of regulation are finding themselves at a disadvantage. As a result, financial centers whose success in the past rested on light regulations may find it hard to compete in the future. They will have to make difficult strategic decisions to either implement regulations according to international best practice or risk getting marginalized.

c. Availability of Talent

A basic condition for success of the financial centers is the availability of a talent pool that is deep and multinational. Professionals with certain technical skills need to be available in order for activities to take off, these include bankers, traders, qualified accountants, auditors, lawyers, risk managers, IT specialists, administrators, and telecommunications experts among others. If the local talent pool is insufficient, or certain skills were found to be lacking, financial institutions should be allowed to attract talent from abroad and the host country is called upon to facilitate visa and residency requirements. Successful financial centers, whether New York, London, Hong Kong, Geneva or Singapore, all have deep and multinational talent pool to draw upon. The establishment of the core financial services in the center will have to be complemented with other related professional activities in order for the financial hub to grow and prosper.

d. Quality of Life

Quality of life is important for highly paid professionals, whether nationals or foreigners. Successful centers are changing constantly to keep delivering the cosmopolitan life style that would attract and retain the required talent. This includes the availability of high quality housing, schooling and health care, as well as, cultural and recreational facilities, entertainment and shopping centers, international air links, strong telecommunication networks, hotels, wide spread internet connectivity, good infrastructure, efficient government services and above all security and political stability.

Another important factor is to have a friendly tax environment that encourages investments and eliminates double taxation. The financial center should provide sound exchange rate regime, and have open access to domestic and international markets.

6.3 Financial Centers in the MENA Region

There are four financial centers in the MENA region; all of them are in the Gulf. These are Dubai International Financial Center (DIFC), Qatar Financial Center (QFC), Bahrain Financial Harbor (BFH) and King Abdullah Financial District in Riyadh (KAFD). Only Dubai features among the top twenty financial centers worldwide in terms of contribution of its financial services to GDP, after New York, London, Paris, Chicago, Tokyo, Shanghai, Hong Kong, Singapore, Frankfurt, Zurich and Geneva.

Cities such as Cairo, Kuwait City, Beirut, Casablanca, and Amman have well developed financial services sectors, but cater primarily to their home market rather than to the regional or international market.

In September 2004, the Dubai International Financial Center (DIFC) started operations, followed by Qatar Financial Center (QFC) in May 2005, Bahrain Financial Harbor (BFH) in 2009 while the King Abdullah Financial District (KAFD) in Riyadh became operational in 2015.

a. Dubai International Financial Center (DIFC)

The DIFC is an offshore financial market, which has its own jurisdictions, trades in US dollars only, and has a tax exemption for 50 years. In September 2005, the Dubai International Financial Exchange (DIFX) was established that was later branded Nasdaq Dubai, reflecting the cross holding of its two partners, Bourse Dubai and Nasdaq stock exchange of New York. DIFC has an independent regulator, the Dubai Financial Services Authority (DFSA), which draws on laws and regulations from the US, the UK and Canada incorporating international best practices.

The number of active registered companies within the DIFC reached 1,225 by end of 2014. The year saw an addition of 242 new companies including 35 financial services firms and 40 retail outlets taking the total to 145 active retailers and 682 non-financial services firms. The combined workforce of companies registered with the DIFC stood at around 17,860, representing 131 nationalities. DIFC is today the location of choice for 22 of the world's top 30 banks, 11 of the world's top 20 asset managers, 7 of the top 10 insurance companies and 7 of the world's top 10 law firms.

DIFC's increasingly diverse mix of clients is reinforcing its growing reputation as the gateway between East and West. The Center currently hosts 385 financial firms from across the globe, including 35% from Europe, 30% from the Middle East, 14% from North America, 12% from Asia and 9% from the rest of the world. In December 2013, the government of Dubai enacted the amendment of several DIFC laws and regulations in order to comply with the requirements set out by the OECD Global Forum on Transparency and Exchange of Information for tax purposes, and aligning the arbitration law to the New York convention.

The increasing number of clients, in addition to the internal expansion of companies already existing within DIFC, has contributed to significantly high occupancy rates within the Center. As of 31 December 2014, occupancy of DIFC-owned commercial offices in the Gate District (Gate Building, Gate Precinct and Gate Village) reached record highs of 99% of leasable space (total commercial office space of 1.3 million square feet), and 99% occupancy rates of DIFC-owned retail space (total retail space of 282,000 square feet).

To meet the growing demand in DIFC, around 877,553 square feet of Gross Floor Area of space was made available in the Center, in the form of the recently opened Daman offices. Office space is also available in other third party owned and managed properties including the index tower, Park Towers and Emirates Financial Towers. The combined space available in these buildings would allow DIFC to accommodate and additional workforce of 15,000.

There were several "soft infrastructure" developments in the past few years, such as the introduction of framework for institutions to develop sharia-compliant products and services, thus ensuring Dubai will become an Islamic Finance hub. Going forward, DIFC is planning to concentrate on the development of such financial services as Islamic finance, fund management, capital markets and, family businesses. DIFC is also planning to expand into new growth markets such as Africa, the Indian Subcontinent and the CIS countries. This will help provide additional business opportunities to firms based both within the DIFC and the wider region. Dubai has become the third largest global center for Sukuk following the recent listing of Sukuk from the UK, Hong Kong, South Africa, and ABC Bank of China. The total value of listed Sukuk on Nasdaq Dubai reached $25 billion by end of 2014.

DIFC also has the intention to become one of the world's leading fund management centers, competing head on with Luxembourg and Dublin. A collective investment law was introduced that covers all asset management activities including mutual funds, property funds, Islamic funds, hedge funds, funds of funds and private equity funds.

The proposed new Qualified Investor Exempt Fund regime is aimed at high net worth professional investors who are knowledgeable and experienced. The minimum subscription is proposed to be $1 million, with a maximum of 50 investors.

b. Bahrain Financial Harbor

With the outbreak of the civil war in Lebanon in 1975, financial business suffered greatly in the country, which until then was the Middle East premier banking hub. Bahrain at the time took a conscious strategy to offer a new home to Middle East banking business. This was not only helped by the push factor of Lebanese civil war but also by the pull factor of rapidly rising oil revenues, which moved the center of economic gravity of the Middle East from the Levant to the Gulf. While it has played a host to offshore banks benefiting from its proximity to Saudi Arabia, Bahrain also has also developed core strength in Islamic banking. Apart from hosting many Islamic banks and regular Sukuk issuance by the Bahrain government, the Accounting and Auditing Organization of Islamic Financial Institutions established its head office in Bahrain.

However, Bahrain's position as a regional financial center was eroded with the rise of DIFC. Equally important, the ascendance to the WTO of Saudi Arabia and Kuwait and the requirement to comply with its rules, made it possible for many foreign banks, insurance companies and other financial services to receive licenses to operate in Saudi Arabia and Kuwait, taking away "offshore" business from Bahrain. Still, Bahrain had a head start and a well-developed regulatory framework administered by the Bahrain Monetary Agency (BMA), the Kingdom's central bank, which maintains stringent control over the financial industry. The BMA also has a well-developed process for establishing special purpose vehicles (SPVs) that is required for issuance of Sukuk.

The Bahrain Financial Harbor (BFH) is a waterfront commercial complex built to strengthen Bahrain's position as a financial hub for the Middle East, with particular expertise in Islamic banking, insurance and asset management. By attracting regional and international foreign investments, it is hoped that BFH can recapture some of the ground that Bahrain has lost to Dubai, its main competitor in the region. BFH also hosts the Bahrain Financial Exchange (BFX), launched in 2010. It is the first multi-asset exchange in the MENA region, which allows for trading of Sukuks, derivatives and structured products along side conventional fixed income and equities.

Bahrain offers the opportunity to set up businesses without local partners. In the wake of Dubai's debt crisis in 2008, Bahrain embarked on a marketing drive to lure business back from its Gulf competitor. However, the political turmoil in the island of 2011 has dampened such aspirations.

Bahrain's financial sector generates more than 50% of its business from Saudi Arabia. Going forward, this reliance on business from the Kingdom becomes a weakness. Saudi Arabia has made it clear that any financial institution that wants to do business in the Kingdom should establish a presence there. Bahrain is more vulnerable to such a development than are Dubai or Qatar.

c. Qatar Financial Center

Unlike the DIFC, the Qatar Financial Center (QFC) is an onshore market place that only guarantees tax exemption for a period of three years, after which companies operating in the center are required to pay the predominant tax rate of 10%. Since making the strategic choice to allow foreign investment in oil and gas and spending large sums on infrastructure and hydrocarbon projects, Qatar has seen a lot of international financial companies setting up shop in Doha. Qatar has the world's third largest gas reserves, and it is estimated that its gas will last for many decades at planned levels. Hence, Qatar set up QFC with a long-term view towards appealing to project financiers and addressing the economic boom in the country.

Rather than being international, QFC is more geared towards the domestic market and its funding needs. It has not attracted the same number of financial institutions as DIFC, and many such institutions have offices consisting mainly of a representative and a secretary. The aim of foreign institutions is to gain a foothold in the burgeoning domestic market rather than establish a presence for regional expansion.

The fully independent Qatar Financial Center Regulatory Authority (QFCRA) was also established in May 2005 to serve as the center's supervisory body. Qatar established the International Mercantile Exchange (IMEX), which is supposed to be an energy-trading platform, but has not attracted any meaningful business, and the plan to offer energy derivatives has fizzled out.

In 2008 Qatar made a far-reaching technology and management partnership agreement with New York Stock Exchange who took a 25% stake in Doha Securities Market for $250 million. An attempt to apply the advanced regulatory framework of QFC to the overall Qatari market in 2007 has failed, and Doha securities market continues to be regulated by the Qatar Financial Markets Authority. Therefore, the intended role of QFCRA to function as a pacemaker of domestic financial market reform has not yet materialized. However, Qatari authorities reiterated their intention to unify the three regulators merging QFC's regulator, the stock market regulator and the central bank who supervises the local banking industry under one umbrella.

d. King Abdullah Financial District, Riyadh

The vision for the $10 billion King Abdullah Financial District (KAFD) is as grand as the scale on which it is being developed by Riyadh Investment Company. Its backers, the Capital Markets Authority (CMA) and the Public Pension Fund, envisage a global financial hub which will be home to major banks and multinational corporations, supported by a thriving community of legal and financial services firms-along the lines of the Dubai International Financial Center. However, KAFD will not offer tax-free incentives for companies to set up shop, and it is more geared towards the domestic Saudi market.

It is early days for KAFD, and some firm commitments have been made in this regard. The joint Central Gulf Bank, which will supervise the execution of GCC monetary policy, along with the Kingdom's Capital Market Authority (CMA), the stock Exchange (Tadawul), Public Investment Fund (PIF) and Saudi American Bank (SAMBA), are among those who moved their head offices to the district. However, the 900,000 square meters of new prime office space will triple Riyadh's top-end commercial space and it will take a while before the 42 tower blocks become fully occupied.

The new mortgage law and the Saudi government's announcement that it would consider the introduction of a government-owned mortgage guarantee institution similar to Fannie Mae of the US could give a massive impetus to the development of Saudi financial markets, as home ownership in the kingdom is still under-developed.

The Saudi stock market is now open to foreign institutional investors. This will undoubtedly encourage more international financial institutions to establish presence in the Kingdom. The Saudi authorities hope that KAFD will create about 43,000 new jobs for its growing population.

6.4 Changing ownership Structure of Arab Exchanges

Most exchanges in the MENA region were established and continue to operate as state-owned organizations, either as incorporated government-owned companies or as unincorporated state administrative entities. As such, exchanges remain somewhat of an outlier in the world of increasingly privately owned and publicly listed exchanges. The World Federation of Stock Exchanges (WFE) which represents the interests of 57 publicly regulated and largest stock, futures, and options exchanges, as well as central clearing houses, is dominated by privately owned exchanges.

In 2014, only 20% of the WFE member exchanges were organized as not-for-profit entities, i.e. not privately owned either by members or a larger group of shareholders. Significant contributors to this figure are MENA exchanges, including the Saudi Stock Exchange (Tadawul), the largest market in this region. This reflects the history of the emergence of exchanges in the region as governmental bodies, with the exception of the Palestinian stock exchange, which emerged out of a private sector initiative, led by a Palestinian holding company (PADICO).

For now, only the Dubai Financial Market has moved towards a private ownership model: 20% of its shares are listed on the Dubai Financial Market (DFM). At the same time, other markets in the region such as Qatar have moved towards greater government ownership. In 2013, the Qatar Exchange has become entirely state owned, following the purchase of 20% by Qatar Holding as part of a strategic partnership deal signed between the two exchanges in 2009.

While ownership changes are unlikely to affect the interest of retail investors, which in most markets of the region are biggest source of liquidity, they may affect institutional investors. Foreign institutional investors may be encouraged by developments in capital markets in the region (for instance if a large international exchange becomes an investor in one of the Arab exchanges). On the other hand, local pension and social security funds, which so far have been marginal investors in local markets, are in principle positioned to grow and may become more active investors in capital markets. Under this scenario, an exchange, which is seen as part of national financial infrastructure, may attract a greater portion of their investment than a privately owned one.

Further consideration of local circumstances and the suitability of privately run exchanges to local economies at this juncture of their development are necessary. For instance, the current ownership arrangements of exchanges, most of which are closely overseen by the CMAs allow these market authorities to create regulations in a manner that is synchronized with the speed of product development (i.e. derivatives, ETFs, etc.). Close collaboration between exchanges, securities regulators and other market actors is arguably fostered by their common goals, set by their respective governments. These common goals have allowed some markets to position themselves globally through strategic partnerships and mergers (i.e. Dubai Exchange's investment in NASDAQ or Qatar's investment in the London Stock Exchange).

Assuming that these considerations are taken into account, will privatization or demutualization of Arab exchanges contribute to their development? While it might be tempting to answer this question positively, as some exchanges in the region already have, a number of consequences of these transitions need to be taken into account before doing so. In this regard, lessons learned in other jurisdictions are critical to examine both for success factors and for concerns that might have rendered the process less than optimal. Looking outside of the region, empirical evidence suggests that private ownership of exchanges have contributed positively to the exchange performance and wider financial markets development. The share prices of listed exchanges have surged and in several cases have out performed the indices of companies listed on these exchanges.

6.5 Towards Multiple Financial Centers in the Region

With an aggressive marketing campaign for its successful Dubai International Financial Center (DIFC) and the city's lifestyle advantages, Dubai has managed to be widely seen as the leading financial center in the region. However, other financial centers must not be forgotten. Bahrain, the region's oldest offshore banking center, will try to regain market share, especially in Islamic banking where it has long experience and an established regulatory framework. Qatar largely focuses on its domestic energy sector and its project finance needs and has not yet developed a more international profile. Financial liberalization in Saudi Arabia and Kuwait could also pause serious competition to the region's more established financial centers. It remains to be seen whether Saudi Arabia can overcome problems of cultural perception abroad and succeed in attracting international talent for its ambitious King Abdullah Financial District in Riyadh.

The region has the potential to develop into an important niche player in the international financial system. MENA's sovereign wealth funds are always looking for foreign investment opportunities, while local companies are increasingly raising debt and equity and engaging in mergers and acquisitions deals. Multi-billion projects in the region are in need of project finance, while the banking retail market in many fields, such as mortgage financing is still undeveloped. In commodity trading, the region has obvious advantages in energy related items and precious metals, and some of the Dubai-related initiatives have good chances to grab more international market shares going forward. The region is well positioned to benefit from the expansion of Islamic banking on a worldwide scale.

The progress made in individual countries, however, does not contradict the fact that many emerging financial centers still have a long way to go to reach the critical volume, liquidity, levels of maturity, breadth of product choice, capacity and stability of market infrastructure. Market oversight by regulators and supervisors that have been achieved in London, New York or Hong Kong over many years will take time for it to become well entrenched in the region. Nevertheless, it is safe to expect that a financial center like DIFC of Dubai is likely to assume strong regional and possibly also global positions within the next decade.

The region's four financial centers, all trying to get off the ground at the same time, must decide where cooperation is mutually beneficial, and where competition serves their interest best. Inevitably the question will arise as to whether all these centers can survive or if consolidation is more advantageous. The top 20 financial hubs in the world include five centers from the US and eight from the EU: these can be termed "multimarket" in a country or region. This illustrates that models for coexistence with close rivals/neighbors already exist and the challenge of a "multimarket" system is therefore not unique to the MENA region and need not be unsustainable.

In the US, Chicago, Boston and San Francisco all serve their immediate regions, as well as, fulfilling specialist functions within the US financial sector. The major US banks and securities businesses have their head quarters in New York, while Washington houses the specialist legal advisory services upon which the banks depend. Chicago is a major center for commodity trading and Boston has a global reputation in fund management.

In other countries, Switzerland is represented by Geneva and Zurich, Australia by Sydney and Melbourne. The EU bloc has a number of member states in the top ranks. They are, however, dominated by London which is clearly in pole position, serving as the senior market for Europe, while the other centers are either specialist niches (such as Ireland and Luxembourg for bonds) or mainly regional centers (Frankfurt, Paris).

Looking at how these neighbors and potential rivals interact should yield lessons for financial centers of the MENA Region and their potential for cooperation. For example, the US model suggests that specialization is one option for maintaining multiple financial centers. The existence of small, important players in Europe indicates that even when pressured by large dominant players, financial centers can

CHAPTER 7

Financial Markets Providing a Stable Environment for Family Businesses in the Region

7.1 Introduction

The founder of Vanderbilt University in the US, Mr. Commodore Vanderbilt, made a fortune in the field of transportation. When he died in 1877, he was the richest man in the US. In the next six years after his father's death, William Vanderbilt had doubled the family's wealth and became the richest man in the world. However, after 30 years of the death of the founder, no member of his family was among the richest persons in the US, and one of his direct descendants died penniless. When 120 of Commodore's descendants gathered at Vanderbilt University in 1973 for the third generation family reunion, there was not a single millionaire among them.

Global statistics show that family businesses face continuity issues through their generational transitions, with around 80% of firms not surviving the third generation. It has become a common knowledge that the first generation of family businesses makes the money, the second generation preserves it, and the third generation loses it. This is due to three main factors: failure to put in place succession plan and to separate ownership from management, divergence of interest by the second and third generation culminating in disputes among family members, and the difficulty of raising capital when needed to expand activities.

7.2 Challenges Facing Family Businesses

As the family size grows and the shareholding base increases, running the business becomes a challenging issue. There will be pressure put on family businesses to grow more rapidly and distribute cash in order to preserve "the per head wealth" and cater for the needs of all family members. Several issues can arise from absence of proper governance structure. There is a tendency not to separate personal money from what belongs to the business. This may be less of a problem when the founder is alive, or he is the only shareholder, but it is potentially explosive when many family members become shareholders.

Studies also show that for all family businesses, no matter what their size or wealth is, good governance is key. In an increasingly fast moving and global market place, the ability to separate management from ownership and make complex decisions in a timely way is critical to survival. Furthermore, success for families is not just about money, but also about longevity. It is about maintaining harmony among family members allowing each one to attain self-fulfillment. It is also about the impact they have on the communities around them.

The successful families are the ones who define success not simply financially, but in two other ways: sustaining a united sense of family connection and developing competency in each new generation to take the family business forward. Those who know their values and live them day to day are more likely to see long-term success.

Ability to manage conflict among family members would go a long way towards strengthening work relationships and encouraging a rich diversity of opinions. Unresolved conflicts are not only harmful but would put the family and the business at risk. The saying that "the bone is strongest where the break heals" (that is medically true) makes sense here as well. Family businesses should learn not how to avoid conflicts but how to manage them. A well thought of conflict management technique should be put in place to help move faster on decisions and avoid disruptive disagreements.

Another challenge is the ability to raise capital when needed, be it for organic growth, expansion, acquisitions, or for a partial or total cash-out for the founders. In the past, family businesses depended mostly on internal sources of funding. But things are changing now. Capital is available through IPOs on local exchanges or by establishing partnerships with private equity firms. The presence of a deep, adequately regulated and flourishing equity capital markets in the region would make it possible for family businesses to explore new sources of funding beyond the traditional bank borrowing and retained earnings.

There are at least four other reasons why several big firms have defied expectations and stayed under family control. One is that they are often the product of a superbly talented entrepreneur. When founders are alive the combination of their abilities and the freedom they have to run by their own rules often gives them a strong competitive advantage. Even after they are gone, their heirs can keep up the firm's success, simply by continuing to follow the founder's successful principles.

Whether private or public, family firms also tend to take a longer-term perspective. This is true both relative to non-family-controlled public companies, which tend to be obsessed with meeting the demands of investors to maximize short-term profits, and companies owned by private-equity firms, which although able to take a longer view than public firms must still cater to investors who want to sell up for a juicy profit within a few years.

Family firms are also less likely to load up on debt. An obvious exception, and an illustration of why most family capitalists fear debt, is the recent collapse of the Portuguese Bank Espirito Santo. Massive debts turned the family-owned financial conglomerate into one of Europe's largest corporate failures, ending in a state bailout of the bank. A reluctance to borrow may limit growth in good times, but it can make family firms more resilient when the going is tough.

Family businesses also tend to have better labor relations. This may be because workers are readier to believe promises that they will be rewarded for delivering in the long run if such pledges are made by founding families rather than outsider bosses who may be gone in a few years.

If family businesses establish four key competencies: enshrining a value driven vision, establishing a conflict management process, putting in place good governance structure and having the ability to raise debt and equity when needed, they will be better prepared for long-term performance.

7.3 Family Businesses In the MENA Region

About 65% of top companies by revenues in the MENA region are family businesses, compared to 40%-60% in other parts of the world (chart 1). In cases even where firms are publicly listed, families continue to hold a blocking interest. For example some 30% of firms listed on the region's stock markets have more than two directors from the same family on their boards and 20% of board members are related. The region's sustained economic growth over the past thirty to forty years has allowed several family firms to evolve into powerful conglomerates, (e.g. Juffali, Olayan, Al Zamil, Al Futtaim, Darwazeh, Al Ghanim, Kanoo, Nuqul, etc.).

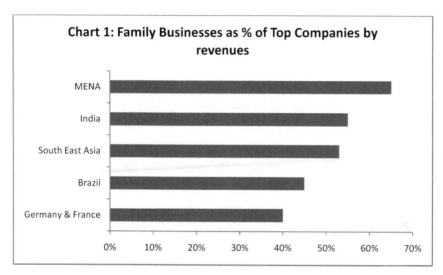

Chart 1: Family Businesses as % of Top Companies by revenues

Source: Economist, May 20, 2015

Industry estimates have placed the overall wealth of family business in the Middle East at $4.5 trillion, with about 35 billionaires. Qatar has the world's highest density of very wealthy families. The majority of high-net-worth individuals in the region, with $2 million or more investible assets are entrepreneurial. Nearly 34% choose to put their money in their own business, while 25% invest in real estate and 16% keep their holdings in bank deposits.

Citizens of Saudi Arabia accumulated the most wealth in the Arab world at $653.3 billion by end 2014, followed by those of the UAE ($461.1 billion) and of Egypt ($389.7 billion). In contrast, citizens of Djibouti accumulated the lowest wealth of $1.9 billion in the Arab world, relative to a net wealth of $4 billion in Mauritania and $23.7 billion in Sudan. In parallel, Qatar has the highest net wealth per capita among Arab countries at $123,682 as at end of 2014, followed by UAE ($91,251), Kuwait ($86,678), Bahrain ($32,668), Oman ($30,021), Saudi Arabia ($23,229) and Lebanon ($20,822). Syria, Mauritania and Sudan have the lowest net wealth per capita among Arab countries of $2,511, $2,148 and $981 respectively.

Family businesses in the region engage in a diverse range of activities, with a typical pyramid corporate structure, where the founder sits at the top and immediate family members form the executive management. The model has been tried and tested and has helped to make family-owned businesses the most important players in the region since 1940s.

Where many family businesses in the West have diluted their holdings from majority to minority stakes, allowing outside professionals to be in the driver's seat, the region's family businesses have yet to fully adapt to the 21st century global corporate culture. There is still, for example, a strong resistance to relinquishing boardroom control and accepting to go public in order not to be subjected to stringent disclosure standards enforced by market regulators.

Trust among family members is valued more than the advantages of increased corporatization and easier access to financing from the capital markets. Financing from traditional sources, mainly retained earnings and banking loans, remains the rule. Family enterprises in the region are reluctant to give up unlimited control and succumb to the increased accountability standards that come with a public listing, like quarterly reports and the appointment of independent directors to the board. Pursuing long-term goals of the family business is put at the center stage ahead of specialization and core competencies, the latter being more appealing to stock market investors. The initiative of NASDAQ Dubai to reduce the minimum free float for its IPOs to 25% was launched with an eye towards such family enterprises, who are hesitant to give up their majority stakes.

Access to loans from banks has become more difficult for many companies, despite the huge credit growth that has taken place in the region. Bank lending has been mainly directed toward a selected minority of large companies and towards consumer financing. The World Bank has deplored the disconnect between the financial sectors and the real private economy in the Middle Eastern countries.

While on the macro level a reasonably high degree of financial intermediation of about 60% of GDP can be observed, it is only few large companies that profit from it, while the majority seems to rely on retained earnings and internal sources of funding.

About 75% of the financing requirements of the small to medium size enterprises (SMEs) in the MENA countries stem from internal sources and only 12% from the banking sector. In Saudi Arabia, for example, less than 40% of SMEs reportedly have an overdraft facility with a bank and only slightly more than 20% have had a loan from a bank. More access to the capital markets could certainly facilitate the expansion and modernization drive of many family companies.

Unlike the western countries where dominant family businesses have moved to the ownership of the third and fourth generation, in most MENA countries, the big conglomerates are still under the second generation ownership, with around 20% starting to see significant involvement from members of their third generation. Upon the passing of the founder, some families have had major conflicts and ended up in courts.

Sharia inheritance laws provide for the estate of the deceased to be granted to his sons and daughters, with males getting a higher proportion of the shares, on a 2:1 basis. Typically, founders give each of their children one or two business lines to run. With the passing of business into the third generation of owners, the tradition of allocating business lines to an ever-expanding number of family members would lead to inefficiency and eventually the dilution of the family conglomerates.

Successful family owned businesses in the region have enjoyed distinct advantages including limited external competition (import substitution strategies) and special access to funding from public sector institutions. The cultural heritage of the region had so far protected family businesses from several major and destructive family feuds. As and example, following the death of the founder, leadership is traditionally passed to the eldest son, a practice typically accepted by other family members. However, this advantage is fragile as families expand and as the gap in experience and knowledge increases among various family members.

With these issues coming to the fore, there is a growing consensus that governance structures need to be overhauled to address issues related to succession planning, separating management from ownership, dealing with family disputes, preservations of family wealth and promoting family business continuity.

7.4 Changing Governance Structures and the Need for Family Council.

Maintaining a balance between family and business issues and separating ownership from management are among the major challenges faced by family firms in the region today. According to several studies, firms in the US and Europe that are family owned or have large family ownership but not managed by family members have done well as they have moved to the second and third generations. Most firms who survived to the third generation were those that had early on put in place formal rules to ensure effective governance structure and proper succession planning (chart 2).

Chart 2: Governance of Family controlled companies covering 2,400 of the Worlds Largest Businesses in the 21st century

1- How many of the Board of directors are non-Family employees?

2- How many voting member does the board of directors have?

3- How many of the voting members of the board are family members
Employed in the business?

4- How many of the voting members of the board are family members
Not employed in the business?

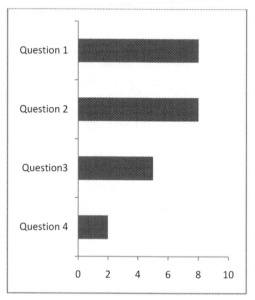

Source: *Ernest and Young, 2015*

The emotional challenges of family business can be overwhelming and the complexity of issues faced would considerably increase, as the number of family members gets bigger. A family council would go a long way towards managing this complexity. However, a clear sense of mission and a defined set of objectives for the council need to be agreed upon by family members in order for the council to be effective. The council should also have a strong leader to set the agenda, keep the council process moving, and communicate to the management board the views of the family members. The family council would in effect become the shareholder general assembly of all family members, which deals with matters of succession, administrative aspects, dividend policy and general business family issues.

The family council would be separate from the management board of the holding company. In this way business issues are dealt with independently from family issues. Shareholders can hold discussions and agree on a vision and then ask the board to take the measures that it deems appropriate to implement this vision.

It is noticed that family members who are active in the business have problems respecting inactive members or understand their role in the business as shareholders. They are unable to separate the emotional from the business issues and often try to use the family council to settle personal conflicts. All these issues need to be addressed early on in order to preserve the effectiveness of the family council.

The work of family council is important and valuable. Families need to realize that building family unity frees the management to concentrate on achieving growth and profitability. When family councils are working well, they help to create a unified voice of the family to give general direction to the board and management.

Experience shows that the surest way to make a family firm prosper once it gets to a certain size is to introduce proper corporate governance. Recent research by Hawkamah, a specialist in corporate governance, shows that families dominate the boards of half of the UAE's listed companies. The founder and immediate family members have traditionally run family businesses in the region with little or no accompanying corporate structure in place. Senior management of these businesses are not accustomed to being accountable to shareholders nor do they accept to have their performance being assessed by board members. Most family businesses resist giving up complete control and refuse to share information with independent board members.

One of the main decisions that a family faces is how to constitute the board. The way forward is to create a two-tier structure, where a handful of family members are chosen by a majority of shareholders as general partners. These general partners select a board, which includes outsiders, serving as independent board members, to supervise management and set strategic direction for the business. The general partners are themselves answerable to the family council, a wider forum, which represents the interest of all family members who are shareholders of the business.

7.5 Funding of Family Businesses

Family businesses in the region had given little attention in the past to alternative sources of funding other than retained earning and bank loans. As they grow they realize that they need more sophisticated financing tools to manage their expansion. This boils down to a choice of going public, approach private equity investments or issuing bonds and Sukuk.

Debt securities have their advantages they can be a relatively less expensive way to raise funding than equity financing and are typically less time consuming to complete. The corporate bond markets in the region have gained enough depth, encouraging family businesses to tap this source of finance. Corporate borrowing costs are lower than at any time since 2007. By the end of 2014, the average yield on S&P MENA bond index was 2.86%, compared to the yield on Emerging Market composite bond index of 5.40%. The yield on S&P MENA Sukuk index was 2.50% reflecting the dominance of Sovereign Sukuk issues in the index. However, the corporate Sukuk market is picking up especially in the GCC, while countries like Jordan, Egypt, Tunisia and Morocco have been finalizing their legal framework to facilitate issuance of Sukuk.

Raising equity based finance is more advantageous than raising debt finance, whether through initial public offering (IPO) or by selling a stake of the company to a private equity firm.

There are several advantages for a family company to go public. These are:

1) Establish a market valuation for the company, which shareholders can see and feel in the financial markets everyday.
2) Establish a quick and fair exit mechanism for some of the shareholders (usually second or third generation family members), who do not wish to remain in the business and opt to do something else.
3) Depending on the percentage ownership sold in the IPO, the original shareholders could also maintain a significant degree of control over the company's operations, which is usually desirable.
4) As a public shareholding company it would have cheaper access to capital (debt and equity), which is often needed for future growth and expansion.
5) By selling part of their business, the owners of the family companies would receive a cash reward for what has often been a generation of hard work. They can invest part or all of the equity raised back into the business for expansion, or use it to finance acquisitions of other companies. Another popular use is to provide them as compensation to incentivize staff.

Companies should take great care to select the capital market that is right for their particular IPO. The first choice is the home market where they are known and recognized. However, for regional companies going public, certain exchanges are more accommodative than others. Some exchanges require a majority of a company's shares to be sold in an IPO, which can result in a family suddenly losing control of its company, while others allow a sale of 25%-30%, leaving the family still with most of the voting rights.

In this region, some exchanges are more open than others to international as well as regional investors. The diversity that is added by international investors can lead to a company achieving price stability as well as fair value for its shares more easily than one that is restricted to mainly local investors.

The corporate governance standards required by capital market authorities also differ from one country to the other. Some insist that listed companies have independent board members and accounts that are scrupulously audited. Meeting the more demanding obligations certainly requires effort, but this can be amply rewarded by more diverse investor base and perhaps improved public perception, with investors and business partners holding the company in high regard because of its transparency and commitment to best governance practices.

Other factors to consider include whether an exchange allows short selling and other hedging mechanisms. Handled responsibly, hedging can encourage institutional portfolios, which would contribute to liquidity and fair value.

Rules affecting minority shareholders are also important, especially for family-owned businesses. Some, called tag along rights, protect minority shareholders by ensuring they can sell their shares at the same price as the majority shareholders in case of a takeover. Others, known as drag along rights, force minority shareholders to sell in a takeover, which can prevent them from blocking a deal desired by the majority.

The rules and environment of one exchange can differ from another, producing a different outcome for the listing. For example, some exchanges allow shares to be sold at market value in an IPO, through what is called a book-building process, while others insist on pricing shares at the book value of the assets, which produces a lower valuation and leaves the original owners with less money.

The book-building model creates a market for the stock before it is offered to the public through a system of bids from institutional investors. A price range is announced based on valuation of the company using discounted cash flow and comparable transaction methods as well as, feedback from research reports. Investors are then asked to indicate the amount of shares they are willing to buy at various prices within the specified range. The orders are captured in a book of demand and provide the basis to price the offering.

If the fixed price approach is to be followed, the leading investment bank would receive subscription applications and funds from investors at the fixed price announced at the launch of the offering. This price is normally based on the net asset value of the company as determined by one of the big accounting firms. The regulator would review the valuation method and approve the price arrived at using this method. The valuation of the company is then divided into a certain number of shares at an established nominal price of say 10 Saudi riyals or 10 UAE Dirhams, etc.

Being a public shareholding company would put the company, its board of directors, and its senior management under stricter disclosure and filing rules of the regulatory authorities supervising the market where the company is listed. Moreover, the research analyst community and investors would continually be monitoring the company and its earnings and growth potential, which could produce volatility in its market price. The demand for full-fledged audited financial statements to be filed every quarter as well as paying the exchange where the company is listed the required annual fees would be an added expense on the company.

Not all family businesses in the MENA region are ready for an IPO. Some require further nurturing in order to upgrade their corporate governance and strengthen their internal controls. Others need equity funding to expand capacity and benefit from economies of scale. As family businesses grow and prosper, they can get stuck with their own corporate culture and their own way of doing business. Selling part of the company to a private equity firm (PE) will be the catalyst that brings the necessary change.

When PE firms invest in a pre-IPO company they will impose higher levels of corporate governance and strengthen internal audit and control. They will also introduce financial planning to help family businesses grow at a more manageable speed. PE firms will use their network and experience to put in place a validated corporate structure, a solid growth strategy and an effective management team. All of this will enhance the valuation of the family business and increase the likelihood of a successful IPO when the time is right to go for a public offering.

Private equity professionals help a family owned company to devise a coherent strategic plan. They design proper corporate performance management processes that ensure control over strategy implementation and devise objective management incentives schemes that are linked to the achievement of business objectives. They would also conduct a detailed review of the organization structure to confirm whether the current structure is optimal for the future business plan and assess the need to bring additional talent on board. They maintain strong networks of industry and functional experts that they can leverage (via executive, board, or consulting capacities) to work on various performance improvement projects.

Private equity investors also help establish proper internal controls and ensure that policy, procedures, information technology systems, and best practices are implemented and appropriately utilized. They institute a strong corporate governance system that encourages shared and independent decision-making. They would offer expert advice on the financial restructuring of the target company, which results in increased profitability and cash flow, coupled with a healthier balance sheet. Additionally, they help the target company build strong relationship with the banks, thus reducing financing costs.

Private equity professionals leverage their local and international networks to support investee companies to grow organically, whether it is through the addition of new products or services or geographic expansion. They would systematically screen the market for potential value adding acquisition opportunities capitalizing on their deal making expertise.

Historically, companies that were partly owned by private equity investors were sold at premiums compared to other family businesses that were not owned by private equity. Private equity professionals possess expertise in navigating through IPO processes, which many family owned businesses lack. In many cases, depending on the growth potential of the company and the size of their retained stake, family business owners can make as much or more from their minority interest as they did from selling their majority interest.

Sometimes, next generation family members are either not inclined to take over or not capable of leading the business through its next phase of growth. Typically, business founders have managed all aspects of the business and this can leave serious gaps when second generation family members assume leadership. Private equity can be an important solution to these business challenges, by taking an objective view of the needs of the business, facilitate critical mediation between various branches of the family business during transition periods and introduce a professional management team to ensure a smooth transfer of control.

7.6 Wealth Management: Developing the Family Office

In the MENA region, the line between running the business and managing the wealth of the family is often blurred, reducing transparency and making it difficult to assess the real profitability of the business. Creating a family office to handle activities ranging from asset management to tax and estate planning will allow management to concentrate on attaining growth and higher earnings. The family office will also take care of such basic services such as property management, accounting and payroll processing, philanthropy, and other concierge type services such as travel arrangements and selecting schools and universities for children.

One of the primary functions of a traditional family office is to consolidate financial management with a view to preserving wealth, generating returns and minimizing the tax impact for any family's fortune. Small teams of professional investment managers are responsible for managing the family's assets and the family office.

Family offices are classified as class A, B or C depending on their administrative structure. Class A family offices, are operated by an independent company with a direct supervision from a family trustee. Class B family offices, are operated by a bank with ample wealth management expertise who can provide better access to market information, equity research and technology. Class C family offices, are directly operated by the family with a small support staff. The majority of family offices in the region could be classified as class C. Having such an office would allow family members to pursue their own careers, while enjoying the benefits of professional wealth management. Table 2 shows the typical asset allocations of family offices.

Table 2

| Typical Asset Allocation for Family Offices ||
Asset Class	Allocation (%)
Equity	35
Fixed Income	30
Real Estate	14
Cash	13
Alternatives (hedge funds, private equity, etc.)	8

A family office often uses trusts as a structure for asset management. Many banks that have developed an expertise in custody have very active and financially profitable trust departments. Trusts can be used as a commercial structure to hold securities (bonds, stocks, etc.) on behalf of the family office, and are extremely flexible and can be tailor-made to suit each case. Control of trust assets is put in the hands of one or more individuals for the use of all beneficiaries. The founder can retain some control over his assets while at the same time assigning them to a trust. After the death of the founder, the assets in the trust will continue to belong to the trust, and creditors will not be able to go after his assets, as they are technically no longer his.

Trusts are useful in tax planning, by replacing high inheritance tax rates on the founder's death with a more favorable tax option. Trusts will help postpone children's access to their funds until they have reached a certain age, and can also protect against political instability. Because trusts do not have a legal entity, it is the trustees who can open bank accounts on behalf of the trust. Where a bank account is opened and management of the funds is delegated to the bank, legal ownership and control of the assets remain with the trust and its nominated trustees.

7.7 Conclusion: The Challenge Ahead

Family businesses in the MENA region are facing several challenges that they need to manage. Ownership of the business and consequently its control will likely become more fragmented as it reaches the third generation. The larger family size will require family business to attain higher annual growth rates in order to maintain the same level of wealth across generations. These businesses can risk decline or possible extinction, or they can create an enduring corporation and lasting legacy for their families. Chart 3 summarizes the key actions that have been identified to drive the successful evolution of a family run business in the region.

1. Re-evaluate the existing business portfolio, creating sharper focus and agreeing on a value driven vision shared by all. This can be difficult, as many families in the MENA region tend to hold on to the traditional businesses for emotional rather than rational reasons. Families must have the discipline to optimize the use of their capital and to target fewer businesses to drive superior performance.

2. Put in place the proper governance structure, separating management from ownership and agree on a well thought of succession plan. This necessitates building managerial capabilities and attracting professionals from within the family or outside it. Inviting highly qualified board members and putting in place a management team capable of growing the business independently of the shareholders. This may require relinquishing control when necessary and introducing the right incentive scheme to attract talent.

3. Apply rigorous discipline when evaluating new investments emphasizing return on capital and explore new sources of funding other than the traditional bank borrowing or retained earnings. These include partnership with private equity firms

and going public by issuing IPO when the time is right. When the family business has matured enough to withstand the scrutiny of regulators and the disclosure required by outside shareholders, then it can consider the option of going public.

4. Establish a family council to help manage conflict among family members, separating the emotional from the business issues. Building family unity would free the management to concentrate on achieving growth and profitability. A family council will help create a unified voice of the family, serve as a general assembly of all family members and give general direction to the board and management.

5. In the MENA region, the line between running the family business and managing the family wealth is often blurred. Creating a family office to handle activities ranging from asset management to arranging travel and philanthropic activities would allow management to concentrate on running the business.

6. Family businesses in the region by virtue of the huge amount of time they spend together have a greater opportunity to help each other identify and promote entrepreneurial activities. A family who wishes to help its members define their vision and reach their goals must not only understand the value of gathering but also commit to spending organized time together perhaps through annual or semi-annual family retreats. Aside from love, respect and core values, the best gift that the senior generation of a business-owning family can offer its children is permission: permission to be who they are, permission to express themselves, permission to try even to fail, permission to discover their passion in life and permission to pursue it.

7. The biggest challenge for family companies is how to preserve family control while competing with public companies that can draw on equity markets. One solution is to stick to a tiny

global niche; many Mittlestand companies (medium size German companies) credit their success with refusing to compete with the big players. A second strategy is to form a close relationship with a local bank. This was once popular with Quaker families in Britain and is still the norm in Saudi Arabia and the Gulf. But the most successful technique is to structure your company so that you can separate the right to a return (income) from the right to a say in how the company is run (control).

The most popular way to do this is by pyramiding. If a capitalist uses his own or his family's money, his scale of operation will be too small. If he raises equity through an IPO, he risks losing control. Pyramids provide him with the best of both worlds: secure control and open access to public capital. The family controls the company that sits on the top of the pyramid, which has a controlling stake of more than 51% in the company at the next level, and so on down the pyramid. This system allows families to maintain the maximum amount of control on companies where they have ownership. Italy's Agnelli family, Sweden's Wallenberg family and Saudi Arabia Olayan family control several companies through pyramid structures.

A second technique is to issue dual-class shares, with the upper class carrying superior voting rights. This is widely practiced in the media world. A family can provide 40% of for one of the company but control 80% of the votes. There are various variations on the two class options, including voting caps on non-family shareholders; cross shareholdings giving families ownership in each others companies and issuance of golden shares that carry specific rights.

Chart 3 : Key Questions Covering the Full Spectrum of the Family Strategy Building

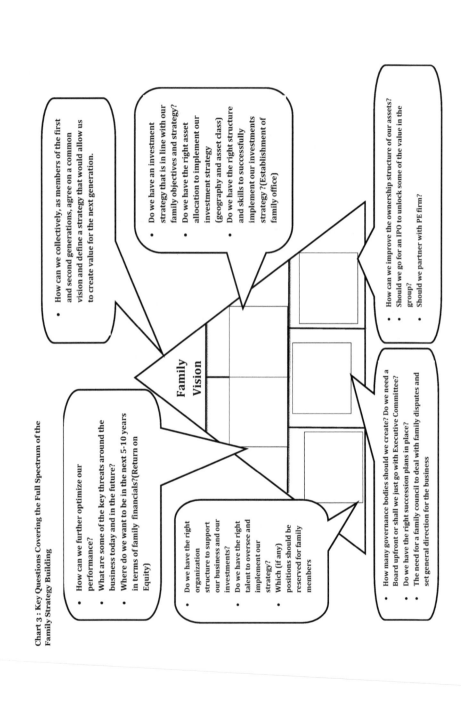

- How can we collectively, as members of the first and second generations, agree on a common vision and define a strategy that would allow us to create value for the next generation.

- Do we have an investment strategy that is in line with our family objectives and strategy?
- Do we have the right asset allocation to implement our investment strategy (geography and asset class)
- Do we have the right structure and skills to successfully implement our investments strategy ?(Establishment of family office)

- How can we further optimize our performance?
- What are some of the key threats around the business today and in the future?
- Where do we want to be in the next 5-10 years in terms of family financials?(Return on Equity)

Family Vision

- Do we have the right organization structure to support our business and our investments?
- Do we have the right talent to oversee and implement our strategy?
- Which (if any) positions should be reserved for family members

- How can we improve the ownership structure of our assets?
- Should we go for an IPO to unlock some of the value in the group?
- Should we partner with PE firm?

- How many governance bodies should we create? Do we need a Board upfront or shall we just go with Executive Committee?
- Do we have the right succession plans in place?
- The need for a family council to deal with family disputes and set general direction for the business

CHAPTER 8

Private Equity: A Sophisticated Source of Growth Capital in the Region

8.1 Introduction: Structure of Private Equity Firms

Private Equity (PE) is intended to be a medium to long-term investment for buy and hold investors. This form of long-term patient capital can be a very valuable asset for companies looking to grow. PE firms are usually privately held, especially those operating in the MENA region. However, in the US, the major PE firms: Carlyle, KKR, Blackstone and Apollo have now become publicly listed companies.

A common criticism of PE funds is that they achieve high returns by leveraging their target and cutting costs, eliminating jobs and destrooften in employment. The study of 527 European-based businesses owned by PE over 2005-2012, shows that PE returns are more than leverage and market returns. For exits in the sample between 2005 and 2012, stock market returns (those from comparable public companies) account for 30%, leverage for less than 35%, while fundamental improvements to the additional business account for over 35% of outperformance. While there is some variation in these percentages from year to year, strategic and operational outperformance has always made up the largest proportion of returns generated by PE in each of the annual studies conducted.

Other studies, using data from a sample of medium-sized manufacturing firms in Asia, Europe and the U.S., show that PE-owned companies are significantly better managed than government owned, family-owned, and privately-owned companies. This is evidenced by more robust operations and management practices, such as the adoption of modern lean manufacturing, continuous improvement and stronger people management practices.

Managers of PE firms are often referred to as General partners or GPs, while investors are known as Limited Partners or LPs. This indicates the limited liabilities of the investors, i.e. investors can lose at most their total capital contribution to one or more of the companies in the portfolio of the PE fund but not their entire wealth. LPs do not influence the day-to-day operations of the fund; management and investment decisions are left to the GPs. Most PE funds have limited lifetime of roughly 8 to 12 years, during which a PE fund typically goes through four stages:

1) Organization and Fundraising: 0-1.5 years
2) Investment: 1-4 years
3) Management: 2-7 years
4) Harvest/Exit: 4-10 years

During the Organization/Fundraising phase, The PE firms follow a top down approach. They identify and study the most attractive sectors/industries. In each sector they look at the entire value chain and decide where they want to be in that chain, then they identify the companies that they want to approach. There are also businesses that come to the PE firm seeking funding, and the GPs will decide which request to accommodate if any.

Fundraising is quite challenging. PE firms do not advertise in newspapers or online to promote their funds, instead the GPs reach out to LPs and other investors they know, including family offices, SWFs and high net worth individuals. Investment banks are sometimes called upon to act as placement agents, and they are usually compensated with 1% on the committed capital they raise.

While LPs make funding commitments to the GPs when they first join the fund, only a portion of their capital is immediately taken by the fund. During the investment stage that ranges from 1 to 4 years, GPs scout investment opportunities and develop deal flows. As more funds are needed for investment they call on LPs to pay from their pledged or committed capital. These requests are termed capital calls.

The drawdown of capital through successive calls allows the GP to maximize the IRR of its investments. IRR is a function of cash on cash return and the time this IRR is generated. By drawing down on capital from LPs when needed, a GP is able to minimize the time element of the IRR calculation.

Beginning in year 2, the PE fund will focus on managing the companies acquired, in some cases replacing the management team with professionals from inside or outside the firm, putting in place a professional board, the right corporate governance structure and adjusting business plan and strategy. The end goal is to create a much bigger, more profitable companies that the PE fund can sell for a profit.

The investments are usually held for a 5-7 years period to give enough time to grow the business before exiting, which is done in one of 5 ways:

1) Trade sale: an outright sale to a strategic buyer.
2) IPO on a local or an international exchange
3) Merger with another company
4) Secondary buyout: sale by one PE firm to another
5) Management Buy Out (MBOs), management will get financing (debt) to buy the company.

Once the company is liquidated, the PE firm distributes the proceeds as follows:

1) LPs receive back their capital

2) LPs receive the hurdle rate of 6%-8% of committed capital
3) Profits are then allocated among LPs and the GP (80% to LPs and 20% to GP). The GPs' 20% is called carried interest. The GP gets as well an annual management fee of 1-2% of committed capital regardless of how their investments perform. The Limited Partners Agreement (LPA) specifies management fees, hurdle rate if any, the split of profits between LPs and GPs, and the lifetime of the fund, among others.

8.2 MENA Private Equity Industry

There are close to 20 PE firms in the MENA region that include the following:

1) Abraj Capital (Dubai)
2) Investcorp (Bahrain)
3) Citadel Capital (Egypt)
4) Eastgate Capital (Jeddah)
5) Amwal Al Khaleej (Riyadh)
6) Gulf Capital (Abu Dhabi)
7) Growth Gate Capital (Dubai)
8) Foursan (Amman)
9) NBK Capital (Kuwait)
10) Euro Mena Fund (Beirut)

The largest is Abraj Capital with $7.5 billion. The total fund raised during the past decade by MENA PE firms reached $20 billion, of which $12 billion have been invested, leaving $8 billion as "dry powder".

Private equity in MENA was not immune to the financial crisis of 2008-2009. When the crisis peaked in fall 2008, PE firms in the region were hardly affected because they scarcely use excessive leverage as a funding method. However, in 2009, fund raising dropped considerably to $726 million raised by 2 funds, from $7.1 billion raised by 18 Funds in 2008. Overall fund raising reached $1.24 billion in 2010 by 7 funds but dropped to $1.05 billion in 2011 (chart 1).

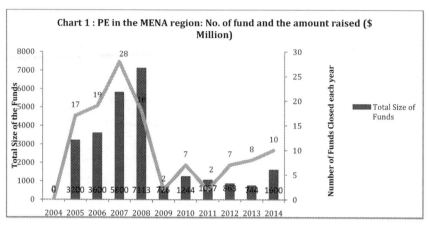

Source: Zawya Private Equity Monitor

The MENA Private Equity Association indicated that private equity funds in the MENA region raised $1.6 billion in 2014, constituting an increase of 65.2% from $744 million in 2013 and compared to $863 million raised in 2012. A total of 10 funds raised capital in 2014 compared to 8 funds in 2013, with the average close per fund rising to $103 million last year from $74 million in 2013. In parallel, private equity funds invested a total of $1.5 billion in 2014 through 72 disclosed investments, compared to $710 million in 2013 through 66 deals in 2013. As such, the average investment size increased to $32 million in 2014 from $15 million in 2013.

The services and education sectors attracted 44% of the total amount invested in 2014, followed by the oil & gas sector with 27%, manufacturing with 11%, food & beverages with 8%, healthcare with 4%, retail with 2% and the information technology sector with 1% of the total. On a country basis, the UAE attracted 55% of the total amount invested in 2014, followed by Saudi Arabia with 21%,

Egypt with 6%, Jordan with 3%, Tunisia with 2%, and Morocco and Lebanon with 1% each. In addition, there were 20 exits from private equity investments for a total value of $1 billion in 2014, compared to 16 exits worth $1.2 billion in 2013. Morocco and Egypt attracted 13 deals each in 2013, followed by Lebanon with 12 deals, Saudi Arabia with 8 deals and Jordan with 7 deals.

The information technology sector accounted for 17% of investment volume by sector during the period 2006-2014, followed by manufacturing and financial services accounting for 10% each, oil & gas, and construction accounting for 9% each, with health care and media & telecom 8% each (chart 2).

Chart 2: Percentage Distribution of PE Investment Volume by Sector (2006-2014)

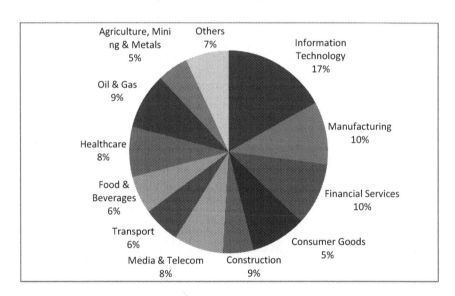

Average investment size remained stable at $8 million, with no increase in 2010-2014, reflecting continuing focus on growth capital and small and medium size investments (SMEs). Buyouts and other large deals of $50 million or more have been rare.

Regional breakdown of PE investments for the period 2006-2014 is given in chart 3. Egypt topped the list of deals by volume since 2006 accounting for 19% of the total, followed by UAE (15%), Morocco (13%), Lebanon (8%), Saudi Arabia Tunisia and Jordan 7% each, and Kuwait (5%).

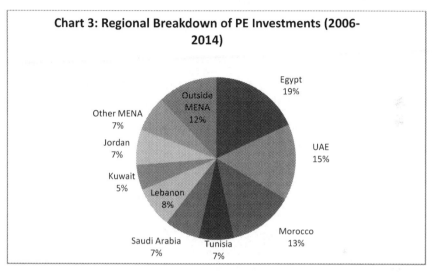

Chart 3: Regional Breakdown of PE Investments (2006-2014)

Egypt 19%
Outside MENA 12%
Other MENA 7%
Jordan 7%
UAE 15%
Kuwait 5%
Lebanon 8%
Saudi Arabia 7%
Tunisia 7%
Morocco 13%

Source: MENA Private Equity Association

The pace at which private equity money has been channeled into new investments appears to be increasing. The Abraaj Group which has $7.5 billion assets under management, closed 10 private equity deals in 2014, almost double its number in 2013. There is definitely more visibility in most MENA countries compared to previous years. The investments are long-term, and PE firms see opportunities and growth beyond the short-term difficulties. Political turmoil in some North African countries and their dependence on the weak European economy have had a negative impact on businesses in that region during recent years. But North Africa have started to attract fresh interest as both politics and the external economic environment stabilized. In April 2014, Abraaj bought a stake in Moroccan chocolate maker Kool Food for an undisclosed sum, and the company closed at least six deals in North African countries in 2014, mainly in consumer-focused sectors, education and healthcare.

Just as important as the increased supply of investor money is the greater availability of routes for private equity firms to exit their investments, whether through strategic sales to companies or through initial public offering of shares. The number of exits completed in 2014 rose to 20 from 16 in 2013, but remained below the 2011 level of 25 exits.

In March 2014, Abu Dhabi-based private equity firm Gulf Capital floated oil service vessel operator Gulf Marine Services in London. The $300 million IPO allowed the company to earn almost 10 times its original investment. It was one of the Middle East's most lucrative private equity exits and a positive signal to the rest of the industry.

Chart 4 : Number of PE Exits Announced Over the Period 2006-2014

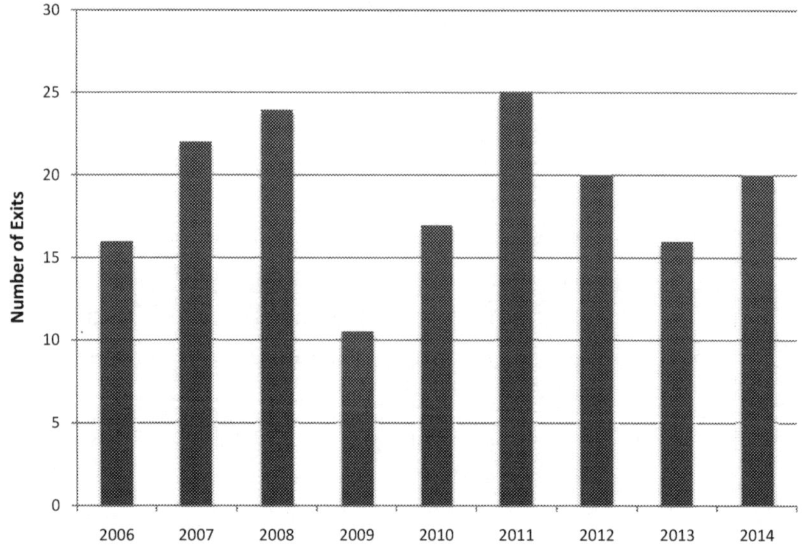

Source: MENA Private Equity Association

Gulf Capital is considering selling other assets in its portfolio, including its 56% stake in UAE-based water treatment company Metito, which was bought in 2007. IPO activity has remained sluggish in most Gulf stock markets since the global crisis, but there are signs of improvement. In 2014, more than 10 IPOs were floated in the region's stock markets. Bahrain's Investcorp, which has made 11 investments through its $1 billion Gulf Fund, will be floating its portfolio's company L'azurde on the public market. Investcorp bought a 70% stake in the Saudi Arabia-based jeweler in 2009.

Although the private equity industry is recovering, the upswing is not expected to be as frenzied as the pre-2008 boom, because fewer players are active. In 2007, at the peak, about 35 funds raised roughly $6 billion. The market has become more disciplined, partly because investors put more emphasis on transparency and corporate governance than they did before the crisis, and partly because banks are not willing to provide financing as freely as they used to do before. Also, some investors have become more sophisticated, they prefer co-investing in specific deals rather than just committing large amounts of money to a fund manager.

8.3 Opportunities for MENA Private Equity

There are a number of characteristics that are unique to the PE industry in the region. One such characteristic is the strong role that LPs play in the PE ecosystem. In developed economies like the US and Europe, the role of LPs is typically limited to providing capital to the GP. In the MENA region, the LPs usually provide their networks for both sourcing and exiting deals. In fact, it is fairly common to see LPs act as buyers in some of the deals.

Another characteristic is the importance of relationships. Strong networks and connections are a key requirements for doing business in the MENA region. This can be explained by the dominance of family owned or controlled business, combined with the cultural factors that emphasize personal connections.

U.S. private equity giant Carlyle had to work out a new model for its business in the Middle East, which is considerably different from its approach elsewhere in the world. In the United States and Europe, Carlyle typically acquires majority stakes or takes full control of companies. But in the Middle East, the most attractive opportunities are those where the owners are not interested in selling control. Instead, they are looking for hands-on partner who can provide growth capital and help them transform their family business into a professional corporation, expand into new markets they may be unfamiliar with, and provide world-class operating practices. Family offices are not interested in selling an enterprise that the family has built over several decades. In the Middle East, the model applicable to most PE firms is to become strategic investors with a strong minority stake of 30%-49%.

Such an approach was used in March 2014, by Emerging Capital Partners (ECP), which agreed to buy 33% of Atlas Bottling Corp, an Algerian firm which bottles PepsiCo drinks, from the local Mehri family. The investment will help to fund an $80 million expansion plan at Atlas, which will increase its bottling capacity, build a new production site and develop new product categories. ECP will give technical assistance to Atlas management.

In May 2015, the private equity arm of Standard Chartered Bank decided to inject $200 million for a 25% stake of Nuqul Group's Fine Hygienic Holdings (Fine), one of the region's largest manufacturers of tissue paper products manufacturers. This will provide growth capital for expansion and enhance Fine's dominant position in the MENA region, leading eventually to an IPO, perhaps within three to five years.

Deals still have the potential to earn higher returns in the Middle East than they would in more developed, less risky private equity markets. Return on investments on PE deals in the Middle East ranges between 20% and 30% annually. This compares to an average of 15% to 20% in more developed markets like the U.S. and Europe.

Another characteristic is that most of the PE firms in the region have historically focused on providing growth capital. Here the PE firms typically invest in "low hanging fruit" opportunities in which the investment is made for a relatively short period of time, with little or no operational change. A brief look at representative transactions confirms this view: many of the largest deals exited in the past decade were characterized by a relatively short hold period. Abraj capital $480 million sale of National Air Services represented a one-year hold (2007-2008). Amwal Al Khaleej's $270 million sale of Dubai Contracting Co. also represented a one-year hold (2007-2008). Citadel Capital's $1.4 billion sale of Egyptian Fertilizers Co. represented a two years hold (2005-2007).

Although the impact of lower oil prices has reduced the number of investments, particularly in the UAE and Saudi Arabia, the GCC countries continue to be the focus of PE firms in the region. The rationale being a continuing increase in per capita income and purchasing power coupled with large demand for infrastructure and high government spending budgets. As Egypt turns back to economic stability, PE deal activity is likely to pick up due to the country's sizeable and growing population, educated middle class, and strategic location. In 2012-2014, Turkey was the most attractive country outside of the GCC region to attract PE investments from MENA Funds due to its large infrastructure expenditure and favorable demographics.

Going forward, more PE activity is expected in major infrastructure projects as governments look for public-private partnerships to overcome funding needs. Demographic-dependent sectors like healthcare, education, financial services and fast-moving consumer goods are attractive in the MENA region, and especially in countries like Egypt, UAE and Saudi Arabia, due to increasing population and a growing middle class.

The absence of excessive leverage makes it virtually impossible for the region's PE firms to conduct multi-billion dollar deals. The regional commercial banks, the traditional lenders for businesses, are not willing to lend any PE firm at a multiple of EBITDA or based on future projections of cash flow streams, unless physical collateral and personal guarantees of the buyers are pledged. The issuance of bonds to finance acquisitions is not a familiar feature of MENA financial markets and the market for mezzanine financing is still at its infancy.

The relatively low taxation, especially in the GCC, does not provide sufficient fiscal incentive for excessive debt financing structures. The focus of PE deals in the region on acquiring strategic minorities rather than full control tends to lessen the need for high levels of leverage. This has erected a safety wall against excessive lending and disciplined the regional PE firms to deploy their equity capital among several investments, with emphasis on strategic minority stakes.

Finally, private equity in the region is falling behind other rival asset classes in the competition to attract Islamic funds. It is estimated that less than 5% of the money raised by PE funds in the region was committed by Islamic investors, even though private equity is as close as one can get to Islamic finance because it is based on real assets. Sharia compliant private equity has failed to take off largely due to sharia regulations that prohibit too much debt financing. Also the long-term illiquid nature of PE investments pose a mismatch to the liquid short-term deposits that Islamic banks hold. In the few deals that were sharia compliant, the PE investment happened in the form of a debt for equity swap, effectively deleveraging the business, being acquired. As Sukuk issuance becomes an important source of long term funding for Islamic Banks, increasingly more funds will be channeled for PE investments, which are mainly of long-term nature.

8.4 Exit Strategies for MENA PE Industry

Since private equity in the MENA region is still in its infancy, only a handful of exits of PE's portfolio companies have been observed in recent years. The data suggests that many of the exits completed during the period 2005-2014 were trade sales, mostly "quick- flips" companies that were sold only 1-3 years after the investment date. The exit routes chosen tend to fit the nature of the underlying business. Although twelve PE-sponsored IPOs were executed during this period, trade sales far exceeded them in value in the ratio of 7 to 1. Only four secondary sales and no management buyouts were completed during the same period.

Most of the PE-sponsored IPOs were listed in Dubai, whether on the Dubai Financial Market (DFM) or Nasdaq Dubai, including Arabtec Holding Co., Aramex Co., Damas, and Depa. Surprisingly there have been no PE sponsored IPOs in the attractive Saudi market. All PE-sponsored IPOs that have been executed to date were below $500 million in value, and most of them were even below $300 million.

Several IPOs of local companies have been listed on foreign stock exchanges such as London (Petrofac, Gulf Marine, DAMAC, Al Noor Hospitals and Al Hikma). Valuation may be a factor affecting local listing whether in terms of rules in certain exchanges or in terms of available peers against which the company will be comparable. Liquidity of listed shares following the IPO may be another factor affecting a decision on local listing. Assessment of listing alternatives in London and the region's stock markets, both market related and regulatory/accounting factors are given in table 1.

Table 1
Comparing Primary Listing on London Stock Exchange With Listing on Regional Stock Exchanges

	London Stock Exchange	Regional Stock Exchanges
1. Strategic Business Sense	International Profile	Regional profile, recognizes historical origin of the company.
2. Depth & Sophistication of investor base	Institutional investors (mutual funds, pension funds, life insurance companies).	Access to local regional investors, mainly retail.
3. Research Coverage	Strong equity research coverage.	Limited equity research coverage.
4. Listed Comparables	Large number of listed comparables.	Fewer listed companies generating some scarcity benefits.
5. Index inclusion	Inclusion in FTSE index and other global indices.	Possible inclusion in MSCI EM index and local indices but no global indices.
6. Corporate Governance	International best practice.	Not yet up to international Best practice.
7. Accounts/frequency of Reporting	Half yearly with quarterly updates. IAS accounts.	Half yearly with IAS Accounts.

8. Pre-emptive rights	Stronger protection of minority rights.	Governed by local regulations.
9. Liquidity	Highly liquid Market.	Less liquid markets.
10. Pricing of IPOs	Price set through a book building process leading to higher valuation.	Usually IPO prices are set below book building process to protect retail investors.

The relative lack of institutional investors remains one of the defining characteristics of the region's stock exchanges. Retail investors still typically account for 90% or more of trading on the region's exchanges. The prevalence of retail investors can also partly explain the limited number of PE-sponsored IPOs historically.

For example, the strict requirements imposed by the UAE regulator, that companies going public have to list at least 55% of their shares through primary, rather than secondary, issuances, prevent PE firms from exiting their investments upon IPO. Additionally, original shareholders are subject to a two-year lock-up period. Nevertheless, these regulatory concerns are found to be of secondary importance to PE firms. The funds are mainly interested in them insofar as they would increase market liquidity, and facilitate new PE-sponsored IPOs. The most important factor is exit and high return.

Trade sales have been the most preferred exit channel for MENA PE firms. Between 2005 and 2014, 45 out of 60 PE exits were trade sales. Trade sales usually lead to higher returns. Looking at all exits between 2005-2014 with published returns reveals that the average IRR was 110% for trade sales compared to 90% for IPOs.

Secondary sale, defined as the sale of one PE firm to another, have been a relatively uncommon type of exit in the MENA region. Buying from a competitor is not viewed as the right way to build franchise.

Besides, the decision to sell to another PE firm may prove problematic when the seller does not have majority control. The majority investor could block the deal or exercise its right of first refusal. What is most important is the fact that PE firms usually offer lower prices when negotiating to buy from another PE competitor, with warrants and lock-ups periods making the process more complex for sellers.

In the MENA region, management buyouts (MBOs) have been virtually non-existent. One key reason for the absence of MBOs is the lack of management sophistication and the fact that creditors are unwilling to back management in leverage buyouts deals.

8.5 Challenges and Opportunities for Private Equity Firms in the Region

The existence of large family offices poses a unique challenge to PE managers in the MENA region. With extensive networks and the ability to realize synergies with existing businesses, family offices are often aggressive and well-funded competitors for PE firms. Even in cases where they are not competing directly for assets, several family offices question the benefits of investing in regional PE funds. Family offices want to diversify their holdings away from the region since the majority of their income is generated by local businesses. They prefer to have flexible investment structures, and can access similar deal flow on their own. Many family offices claim that GPs have not demonstrated consistent value creation capabilities to be credible. Some PE firms have overcome these challenges by emphasizing deal-by-deal fund raising and co-investments, which are more aligned to family office preferences.

Families that have operated a business for several generations may be emotionally attached to the business and enjoy the regular stream of income, and therefore are not necessarily looking for a liquidity event. Business owners are generally against the sale of majority stake but some have embraced minority equity sales in certain situations. Although this limits investors' ability to lever and control the business, many investors have pursued a minority investment model. By negotiating negative control rights and certain provisions in shareholder agreements, PE firms are able to positively influence the performance of target businesses while ensuring that the existing owners are incentivized to improve the business.

Both political instability and the regulatory environment pose significant risk to PE investors in the region. Labor laws are restrictive, minority shareholders rights are difficult to enforce, and business practices are not always transparent. For example, bankruptcy regimes are not well developed, often posing personal recourse risk for management. Furthermore, access to debt financing is typically limited to companies able to pledge hard assets, significantly reducing the use of acquisition financing, a key value creation tool for PE in developed economies. This environment makes it more difficult for PE firms to deploy capital effectively. Finally, many industries are restricted and inaccessible to private investors such as oil and gas and utilities, reducing the potential to diversify PE investments. There are signs, however, that the regulatory regimes are improving, such as ease of doing business, protection of minority rights and developing restructuring laws.

Another concern cited by PE firms is the limited availability of managerial capabilities in the region. In more developed markets, PE firms generally add value by bringing talented managers to the businesses they acquire. Without a stock of managers trained in professional organizations to draw on, PE professionals have to dedicate a significant amount of their time to the portfolio companies. These together, with the unfavorable regulatory environment have forced many GPs to avoid investing in situations that require significant turnaround or overhaul of operations. This reinforces the perception of many family offices that these types of investments can be made directly and do not require expensive PE funds to accomplish.

Finally, PE firms have limited exit options for their investments. There have been few secondary PE buyouts and strategic buyers have shown limited interest in acquiring PE portfolio companies. However, the IPO markets have recently re-opened, especially in the Gulf region, and foreign strategic buyers are showing increased interest in the MENA region.

8.6 Conclusion

The PE industry in the MENA region has concentrated its activities on providing growth capital to existing companies. The majority of PE firms today share the opinion that quick-flips are becoming harder to find. Firms that survived the financial crisis are starting to realize the importance of building in-house operational capabilities that can enhance the portfolio company's bottom line. Focusing on the fundamentals, building specialized operational expertise in select number of sectors, and getting more involved in the management of portfolio companies are necessary factors to continue capturing value from PE investments.

Sometimes family business owners are not willing to invest heavily to drive the business through its next growth phase. In these circumstances, a partnership with a private equity group can provide business owners with peace of mind knowing that they have partnered with competent investors who are looking for ways to bring the business to its next level. As a partnership, the family business can continue to grow and legacy owners can continue to financially participate in that growth without the concern associated with losing control or the need to re-invest more of their own net worth back in the business.

The key priority now of GPs managing private equity fund in the region is to create value and manage risk in portfolio companies and plan for optimal exit. They are focusing on cost reduction, refinancing of existing debt, support on strategic expansion, improving corporate governance, and increasing performance and efficiency from existing assets. LPs are also taking a more active role in the running of portfolio and are insisting on an increase in strategic thinking, and information provision from GPs.

When family businesses in the region continue the transition to third generation owners and start to professionalize management, they are likely to divest non-core assets especially those that are unprofitable. Divested family businesses can be great opportunities for well-connected PE firms to buy such assets on favorable terms.

CHAPTER 9

Venture Capital: Nurturing the Entrepreneurial Spirit of the Region

9.1 Introduction: Structure of Venture Capital Funds

New and small firms find it difficult to obtain debt financing from commercial banks that are generally not willing or able to make loans to new companies with no assets and business history. Instead, startups turn to venture capital funds to get capital financing as well as advice. Venture capital is a professionally managed pool of money used to finance new and often high-risk firms. Venture capital is generally provided to back an untried company in return for an equity investment in the firm. Venture capital firms do not make outright loans. Rather, they purchase an equity interest in the firm that gives them the same rights and privileges associated with an equity investment made by the firm's other owners.

The terms venture capital and private equity are often used interchangeably. However, there are distinct differences in the two types of investment institutions. For example, venture capital firms, generally using the pooled investment resources of institutions and wealthy individuals, concern themselves more with startup businesses, while private equity firms deal more with existing companies looking for growth capital to expand. Further, venture capital firms tend to utilize teams of either scientific or business professionals to help identify new and emerging technologies in which to place their money. Private equity firms draw more on professionals in the fields of finance and management to assess the profitability of existing companies that have already proven themselves in their respective business field.

There are many types of venture capital firms. Institutional venture capital firms are business entities whose sole purpose is to find and fund the most promising new firms. Private-sector institutional venture capital firms include venture capital limited partnerships (that are established by professional venture capital firms, acting as general partners in the firm: organizing and managing the firm and eventually liquidating their equity investment), financial venture capital firms (subsidiaries of investment or commercial banks), and corporate venture capital firms (subsidiaries of nonfinancial corporations which generally specialize in making startup investments in high-tech firms). However, limited partner venture capital firms dominate the industry.

Venture capital firms receive many unsolicited proposals of funding from new and small firms. A majority of these requests are rejected. Venture capital firms look for two things in making their decisions to invest in a firm. The first is high return (sometimes as high as 700% within five to seven years) to take on the high risk associated with new and untested small firms. The second is a clear exit strategy. Venture capital firms realize a profit on their investments by eventually selling their interests in the firm. They want to see the prospects for a quick and easy exit opportunity when the time comes to sell.

Investments by venture capital (VC) funds in start-up companies worldwide totaled $86.6 billion in 2014, constituting an increase of 58.6% from $54.6 billion invested in 2013. Also, a total of 7,474 VC deals were announced in 2014, down by 11.1% from 8,406 transactions in 2013. The number of VC deals in North America accounted for 61.5% of global VC transactions, followed by Europe (19%), China (6.7%), India (5.5%) and Israel (1.7%), with the rest of the world accounting for the remaining 5.6% of total transactions.

VC funds in North America invested $53.9 billion in start-up companies worldwide, equivalent to 62.2% of total VC investments in 2014. They were followed by VC funds in China with $12.8 billion

(14.8%), Europe with $9.2 billion (10.6%), and India with $5.4 billion (6.2%). In parallel, the Internet sector attracted 28% of total VC investments in 2014, followed by the software and telecom sectors with 17% each, and the healthcare industry with 15%. In volume terms, the Internet sector accounted for 26% of the total number of VC deals worldwide in 2014, followed by the software sector with 20%, and the telecommunications and healthcare sectors 15% each.

The VC industry's average annual return improved to 25.9% in 2014. Investments by VC funds in start-up companies totaled $43.9 billion in 2007, $45.2 billion in 2008, $34 billion in 2009, $45.2 billion in 2010, $61.3 billion in 2011 and $52.7 billion in 2012.

9.2 The Ecosystem for Innovation

All humans are born with an innate desire to create. It is an instinct that one can observe in children constructing miniature objects with Lego sets, or toddlers drawing creatively on the iPad. Some are lucky enough to exercise such instincts as adults working in creative jobs or starting new ventures. But many intelligent and ambitious young people never pursue such a path in their careers. The majority of the finest youth in the region are attracted by the money and prestige of the well-paid professions, such as banking, law, consulting, engineering and medicine among others.

Successful entrepreneurship requires a policy environment in which it is possible to start a business, secure funding for it and generate exit. It also needs a supportive culture, where it is acceptable to take risks and fail and where training and mentorship are available for those who have the will and the courage to start something new. Innovation does not have to be transformational (creating the next iPhone), it can be incremental (a new way to reach a customer), or disruptive (a new product, service or a business model). However, the world is filled with new ideas, the challenge is to turn an innovation into something valuable that creates wealth and new jobs. Studies show that during the period 2004-2014, new ventures that account for 4% of the world's private businesses, have created 40% of its new jobs.

It is exciting to note that an "entrepreneurial explosion" is taking place worldwide. Digital startups are bubbling up in a variety of products and services. They are reshaping every industry and changing the way people interact and do business. This global movement has generated a sizeable startup colony, called ecosystem, supported by hundreds of startup schools called accelerators. All these ecosystems are highly interconnected. Information about how to do a startup has become more accessible and more uniform. Global standards are emerging for all startups, from programming tools to term sheets for investments, making it easier for entrepreneurs to draw on these building blocks.

Some of these building blocks are sets of code that can be copied free from the Internet, along with easy-to-learn programing frameworks (such as Ruby on Rails). Others are services for finding developers (ELance & oDesk), sharing code (GitHub) and testing usability (UserTesting.com). Yet others are "application programing interfaces" (APIs), digital plugs that are multiplying rapidly. They allow one service to use another, for instance voice calls (Twilio), maps (Google) and payments (PayPal). The most important are "platforms", services that can host startups' offerings (Amazon's cloud computing), distribute them (Apple's App Store) and market them (Facebook, Twitter). And then there is the Internet, the mother of all platforms, which is now fast, universal and wireless. Startups are best thought of as experiments on top of such platforms, testing what can be automated in business and other walks of life.

Economic and social shifts have provided added momentum for startups. The world economic crisis of 2008-2009 had caused many millennials (the generation that hit young adulthood around the year

2000) to abandon hope of finding a conventional job. They grew up well with technology and embraced its speedy evolution. So much so that many of them probably prefer high speed Internet to high quality air. According to a recent survey of 12,000 people aged between 18 and 30 in 27 countries, more than two thirds see opportunities in becoming entrepreneurs. Young people all over the world see success stories in other places and want to become entrepreneurs themselves.

Another major shift that millennials adopted was their shrinking affinity for assets and the way they approach work and careers. At their current age millennials are less likely to buy property than older generation, staying free from heavy loans or assets that may hamper their global mobility. The rise of on-demand economy, where Uber provides chauffeured taxis, Handy Supplies cleaners, SpoonRocket delivers restaurant meals to your door, Medicast provides doctors ready to be at your home in two hours, Instacart keeps your fridge stocked and Airbnb provides apartment for short term stay.

The world is increasingly being divided between people who have money but no time (time-starved) and people who have time but no money (job-starved). The on-demand economy provides a way for these two groups to trade with each other, at a time when "transaction cost" of using an outsider to provide a service is falling thanks to technology and cheap computing power.

The on-demand economy gives consumers greater choice while letting people work wherever they want. Society gains because idle resources are put to use (most Uber cars would otherwise be parked in the garage). Millennials look for less structure and more fulfillment. Unlike their parents, they prefer to work in a startup rather than in an office or in a career-oriented job.

An important part of the ecosystem, on which venture investments can be established, is to have a stable political environment combined with a strong legal infrastructure that speedily addresses corporate, shareholder, taxation and intellectual property concerns. Another challenge is social acceptance and change. A government cannot create, but only support entrepreneurial drive. For example, while Japan leads the world in filings of intellectual property, the country has the lowest score for entrepreneurship of any large country, mainly due to its risk averse orientation. Bankruptcy in Japan is socially degrading and in the extreme leads to suicide.

The ecosystem for innovation is evolving in many Arab countries. Nevertheless, legal and regulatory framework, financial markets, investment banking, intellectual property foundations and exit opportunities are still nascent and unpredictable, compounding the risk for new ventures. At the grass-root entrepreneurial level, the burning desire to start companies that could change the world has not yet surfaced. The legal complexity of giving new hires stock options and free shares remains generally prohibitive. This limits the entrepreneurs' ability to attract people into a risky career move.

Most Arab countries treat honest insolvent entrepreneurs more or less like fraudsters, though only a tiny fraction of bankruptcies involve any fraud at all. Some countries keep failed entrepreneurs in limbo for years.

There are few less adventurous venture capital firms who are more likely to invest in an idea that has been successful in other regions than take a risk with a completely new concept. Even in the US, and despite all the due diligence, it is estimated by Harvard Business School that 62.4% of venture capital investments were completely lost while 3.1% of the investments accounted for 53% of the profits for roughly 600 investments.

The Global Innovation Index for 2014 ranked the UAE in the first place among 14 Arab countries and in the 36 place globally (table1). Saudi Arabia, Qatar, Bahrain and Jordan followed in the 2nd, 3rd, 4th and 5th place respectively. The index measures innovation in broad sense and includes scientific innovation as well as social and business innovation. It rates the innovation level of each country on a scale from zero to 100, with a score of 100 reflecting the most innovative economy. The index is a composite of 81 variables that are grouped into two sub-indices, the Innovation Input Sub-Index and the Innovation Output Sub-Index. The countries included in the index represent 92.9% of the world's population and 98.3% of global GDP. The index is co-published by Cornell University, the INSEAD Business School and the World Intellectual Property Organization.

Table 1

Global Innovation Index 2014			
	Score	Arab Rank	Global Rank
UAE	43.2	1	36
Saudi Arabia	41.6	2	38
Qatar	40.3	3	47
Bahrain	36.3	4	62
Jordan	36.2	5	64
Kuwait	35.2	6	69
Oman	33.9	7	75
Lebanon	33.6	8	77
Tunisia	32.9	9	78
Morocco	32.2	10	84
Egypt	30.0	11	99
Algeria	24.2	12	133
Yemen	19.5	13	141
Sudan	12.7	14	143

Source: INSEAD.

The average score for the Arab countries in the Innovation Input sub-index was 39.7 lower than the global average score of 42.8 and the average score of the Upper Middle Income countries (UMIC) of 40.6 (table2). This sub-index measures the elements of the national economy that enable innovative activities such as institutions, human capital and research, infrastructure, market and business sophistication.

Table 2

Components of the 2014 Global Innovation Index			
	Global Avge Score	Arab Avge Score	UMIC Avge Score
Innovation Input	42.8	39.7	40.6
Institutions	62.5	58.4	58.9
Human Capital & Research	31.0	29.8	29.6
Infrastructure	37.1	37.7	36.4
Market Sophistication	50.2	43.8	47.3
Business Sophistication	33.3	28.8	30.9
Innovation Output	31.0	24.9	28.9
Knowledge & Technology Outputs	29.2	21.7	26.9
Creative Outputs	32.8	28.1	30.9

Source: INSEAD.

As for Innovation Output sub-index, which reflects innovative activities such as creativity, knowledge and technology, the average score for the Arab countries was 24.9, lower than both the global average of 31.0 and the UMIC average of 28.9. Switzerland and the US had the highest innovation levels world wide with an average score of 65.

9.3 Building Startup Accelerators In the Region

People may differ on what variables create the best ecosystem for startups, but there is a general consensus over the basic ingredients.

A great ecosystem is about a platform that would attract the best and smartest ideas and talents, and facilitate the interaction of entrepreneurs, investors and mentors with lawyers, marketing, accounting, and human resources. In short, they are communities of support aimed at breeding a culture of excellence.

There are several challenges that need to be addressed when building startup ecosystem in the region. Regulatory issues, which vary by country, are often at the top of the list. The uneven and inconsistent application of the law can discourage investors from taking minority stakes in a company. Most of the regulation is pre-emptive, solving problems before they occur, because they cannot be solved in a speedy manner in courts. Bureaucracy remains a major hindrance; in several countries in the region it takes weeks, if not months, to issue new stocks for startup companies.

Broader cultural challenges also exist. Arabs are generally risk averse, preferring to invest conservatively and in hard assets like property rather than in digital ventures. They like to show how successful they are by pointing to their latest apartment building or hotel or manufacturing plant. The whole concept of venture capital is that few ideas will succeed with time, while the majority will fail. Arabs like Japanese do not tolerate failure. It is socially unacceptable for a new venture to fail and bankruptcy should be avoided at all costs.

Up until recently, there has been a shortage of seed or early stage funding beyond the initial personal/family funds raised by the entrepreneurs. Innovators have typically faced a "harsh desert" after starting work on an initial idea whether in terms of seed funding, help and knowhow and supporting environment. Interim capital has also been missing, what is known in the US as the second and third round funding. On the other hand growth capital for later stage funding is available, mainly from several private equity funds that raised billions in the past decade. It is unfortunate that such capital has recently been relatively idle, not finding suitable deals to be deployed in.

Several funding institutions have been established in different countries of the region that aim at enabling early stage companies to transform innovative ideas into viable businesses, and to provide second and third stage funding for the successful ones. For example Flat6Labs was established in Egypt in 2011 based on incubator/ accelerator models in the US. Each quarter, a new cycle commences, where the management team of Flat6Labs selects up to seven startup concepts from hundred of candidates that apply online. Flat6Labs seeds each investment with Egyptian pounds equivalent of $10,000 to $15,000 in exchange for 10% to 15% ownership of the company. The selected teams are hosted in Flat6Labs headquarters. Each week they discuss their progress internally and at the end of the cycle they present their ventures to outside investors (angels). Once the company completes its cycle, it has to move out of the space, with or without backing. Since its inception and till the end of 2014, Flat6Labs has operated six cycles and invested in 50 companies, most of which have gone on to raise second and third rounds funding.

Among the first startup accelerators in the region is Oasis 500. It was established in 2010 in Amman, Jordan under the guidance of HM King Abdulla, with a committee of leaders in the ICT, Digital Media and Venture Capital community in Jordan and the region. Oasis 500 not only provides seed capital for startup companies but also adds value by offering investors intensive training (boot camp) on business management, fund raising, and stress testing among others. Selected entrepreneurs will be given a first round of funding of around $30,000, for a 10% ownership with a possible follow on investment of up to $70,000. Funded companies will be incubated at Oasis 500 for 100 days. During this period they will be provided with guidance and follow-up, coupled with valuable mentorship from industry leaders. Oasis 500 operates an angel network to attract investors to well prepared opportunities, and facilitate second and third rounds of funding for successful ventures. Oasis 500 may coinvest in some of these deals if deemed appropriate. By the end of 2014, 125 companies had completed the incubation and went on to raise second round funding. The six stages of activities of a typical accelerator in the region are given in chart 1.

Chart 1: Stages of Operations of a Typical Accelerator in the

MENA Region

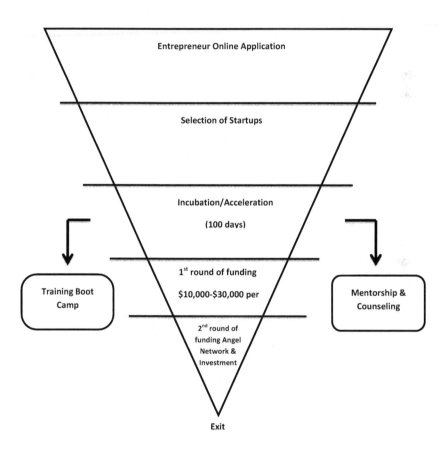

Entrepreneur Online Application

Selection of Startups

Incubation/Acceleration

(100 days)

1st round of funding

Training Boot Camp

$10,000-$30,000 per

Mentorship & Counseling

2nd round of funding Angel Network & Investment

Exit

One of the most important ecosystem builders in the region is the Riyadh based National Net Ventures (N2V), comprised of 25 independent companies in several Arab countries and over $700 million in annual revenues. N2V finds and launches companies by providing entrepreneurs with salaries, seed funding and three to six months of mentorship, and furnish them with shared services like technology, legal and accounting support. N2V usually take a majority stake in the new ventures and give management partial equity in the firms they run.

Seeqnce, Berytech, BIYAT and AltCity are the most active incubators on the Lebanese scene. AltCity is more oriented to social entrepreneurship and its goal is to maximize community engagement. Seeqnce established in 2010, aims to build sustainable startup ecosystems across the MENA region. It offers a virtual platform "Alice" where entrepreneurs sign up and present their ideas to seek advice from professionals and look for partners and financing. It offers an incubation/accelerator program of six months specializing in web/mobile activities. It invests $70,000 per startup for 30% equity with 10% buyback option based on performance and has the right of first refusal for follow on rounds.

Berytech is the oldest incubator in Lebanon, established in 2007 with emphasis on technology and health. It has its own active fund of $8 million and invests $100,000-$120,000 in startup companies for up to seven years. The incubation process of Berytech allows project holders and young startups to benefit from Business Counseling while being physically hosted on the premises. Moreover, a mentor closely accompanies new ventures for the duration of their incubation period, throughout which they will benefit form management and budgets follow up (see chart)

Pre-Incubation	Incubation Services	Creating Viable Businesses
• Project Assessment • Ideas Elaboration • Rough Business Plan • Entrepreneurial Training	• Hosting in managed space • Business counseling • Help with technology & customers • Help with business plan	• Hosting • Networking • Helping In Financing • Marketing

The venture capital firm Middle East Venture Partners Holdings sal (MEVP) announced in November 2014, the IMPACT Fund's first closing, with investor commitments of $56 million. Initially launched in December 2013, the IMPACT Fund is the first venture capital fund to be established as a result of the Central Bank of Lebanon's Intermediate Circular 331 that was issued in August 2013. The circular authorized commercial banks operating in Lebanon to invest up to 3% of their private funds in the capital of start-up firms in the knowledge economy, with a 10% limit per firm of this percentage. The fund plans to invest between $0.5 million and $5 million per firm in Lebanese knowledge-based startups, mainly in the information & communications technology sector and in other creative industries. The fund has set a timetable of up to five years to invest its capital.

In parallel, the fund's investment committee approved five investments for an aggregate of $12.5 million. The fund invested $3 million in Mobinets, a telecom software provider that specializes in next generation smart Operation Support Systems solutions. It also committed $2 million to Fuel Powered, an online platform with multiplayer functionalities that allows mobile gamers to compete with each other, and pledged an undisclosed amount to Fadel Partners, a provider of intellectual property management software and solutions. The fund also announced a $1.5 million investment in Klangoo, the owner of Magnet, which is a text analysis technology. Further, it invested $4 million by the end of 2014 in Bookwitty, an international online book distribution company.

Plug and Play (PnP) of Egypt is the regional offshoot of Plug and Play Tech Center, the Silicon Valley incubator, PnP Egypt sends handpicked companies from Cairo to acceleration programs at its headquarters in Sunnyvale, California. Through its Rising Tide Fund, MENA startups can apply for anything from $10,000 of seed capital to test a new business model to $1 million for a more advanced venture.

Digital-media entrepreneurs from anywhere in the world can apply to Seedstartup, to take advantage of this UAE accelerator and seed venture funds, but are required to live in Dubai during the three-month crash course. Selected startups receive up to $25,000 in exchange for a flat 10% equity stake, and the possibility of another $250,000 when the fully incubated idea is pitched to a global network of potential investors.

Tenmou is based in Manama, Bahrain and it is the country's first business angels company. Tenmou does not offer workspace, but does provide seed financing-typically $50,000 in return for an equity stake of 20%-40%, and three months of intensive mentorship to successful local applicants.

Wamda.com and ArabNet have contributed to developing the region's ecosystem by informing, connecting and improving the talent pool. Wamda.com is now the must read and shared web experience for the region, reaching hundreds of thousand of viewers a month and growing rapidly. Entrepreneurs love the coverage and investors take note of what is happening. Content is one of the three legs of Wamda, the second leg is Wamda Capital, a fund to invest and raise additional money for successful startups. The third leg is Wamda card, offering discounts on basic services to entrepreneurs, ranging from office supplies to travel. ArabNet is the largest summit for technologists and startups in the region, covering such themes as the future of mobile, cloud computing, e-commerce, how to raise money, hire the best talent etc.

9.4 Crowdfunding of MENA Ventures

The latest sources of funding for new ventures are the crowdfunding platforms that allow startups to raise money directly from the general public. Anyone with a convincing idea can ask the crowd for small sums of money which when added can bring the targeted amount. It is estimated that $6 billion were raised worldwide from crowdfunding in 2014, up from $4 billion in 2013, $2.8 billion in 2012 and $1.5 billion in 2011. There are over 450 crowdfunding platforms globally, up from 100 in 2007, with Kickstarter, and Indiegogo of the US being the largest two.

By channeling finance to projects that would typically not receive attention from more traditional funding sources, crowdfunding can contribute to solve the structural gap present in the financing of early-stage ventures. Some see crowdfunding as the next development of popular capitalism, where small investors search for projects and distribute small amounts of their savings across several of them. Currently, however, high-net-worth individuals and professional investors remain the main funders of equity for startup ventures.

Angels are also playing a bigger role in funding startups. By the end of 2014, AngelList, originally a social network for startups and investors, had 24,000 accredited investors, people with a net worth more than $1 million or income of more than $200,000 a year. These investors had put $250 million into more than 1,000 startups of the total 85,000 listed on the site. Venture Capital will continue to play an important role in channeling money to startups; however, many weaker funds will not survive. Crowdfunding will be the future of how most small businesses are likely to be financed.

Crowdfunding in the region is still in its early stages of development. Based in Beirut, Zoomaal is the first crowdfunding platform for startups in the Arab world. It was launched in July 2013, and was backed by Sawari Ventures of Egypt, National Net Ventures in Saudi Arabia, Wamda Capital of Dubai and Middle East Ventures from Lebanon. Having investors and board advisors in different countries maps neatly to Zoomaal's overall strategy of helping businesses gain access to venture capital all across the Middle East. Zoomaal often provides project owners with recommendations of how to crystalize their business ideas. They also hold weekly seminars where they share best practices on growing and engaging a crowdfunding community.

For now crowdfunding seems to have struck a chord with the Arab world. What would be instrumental is the fact that the region is catching up with the rest of the world in terms of Internet usage, along with smart phone penetration and e-commerce (chart 2).

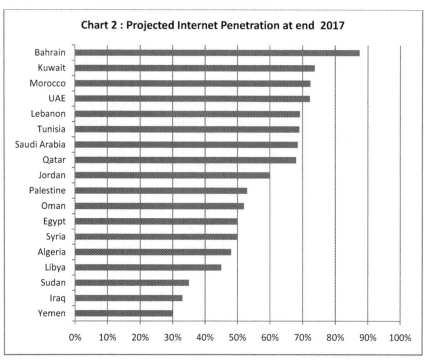

Chart 2 : Projected Internet Penetration at end 2017

Source: MADAR Research & Development, Dubai, UAE.

The Dubai based ICT market research MADAR projected the number of Internet users in the Arab world to grow at a compounded annual growth rate (CAGR) of 11.2% during the period 2012-2017 to reach around 200 million or 51.4% of total population in 2017 from 31.9% at the end of 2012. Internet penetration rate, or the number of Internet users to total population, in the GCC region would rise to 66.8% at the end of 2017 from 53.6% in 2012, while in the Levant region the Internet penetration rate would rise to 50% from 28.5% respectively. Bahrain will have the highest Internet penetration rate in 2017 at 87.4%, followed by Kuwait (73.7), Morocco (72.4%), UAE (72.2%), Lebanon (69.2%), Tunisia (69.0%) and Saudi Arabia close to 68.5%.

The Dubai based crowdfunding platform Eureeca received regulatory approval from the UK's powerful Financial Conduct Authority (FCA), which should give a major boost to MENA startups and early stage businesses seeking investment. The FCA approval means startup companies will be in a better position to attract funding from UK investors and to direct funding to UK based companies. Similarly, the approval will help attract other global investors outside of the UK due to the safeguards and assurances provided by the regulatory body.

With the new regulation and the credibility it provides, Eureeca will become more appealing to institutional investors and family offices will open doors to funding larger SMEs with bigger requirements. Eureeca is the largest angel investor network in the Middle East and is the first online equity crowdfunding platform established outside the UK to receive the FCA approval. The crowdfunding platform had by the end of 2014 successfully funded 12 businesses of different sizes across a variety of sectors since it was established in 2012. In total, approximately $2.5 million had been raised via the Eureeca platform.

Regulation has a key role to play in allowing crowdfunding to develop and protect investors. Existing securities regulation does not reflect the specificities of crowdfunding. Instead, a specific framework is needed that ensures the integrity of platform operations, adequate due diligence to mitigate the potential for fraud and a high level of transparency towards investors. Some Western countries have opted for requiring retail investors to review educational materials before being able to invest.

Without sufficient safeguards of investors, crowdfunding will not thrive. Platforms need to ensure that investors understand the risks and potential losses, while effectively protecting them from fraud. Otherwise, investor damage will quickly turn into lost trust, missing the opportunity to invigorate entrepreneurship and innovation.

9.5 How to Value Startups

While valuation is one of the important ways to assess startups, however, there is no simple method to calculate valuation at the seed and early stage of investments. "Sounds about right" is often an expression used by practitioners when numbers are tossed around. Depending on the stage of the company, valuation can be a simple back-of-the-envelop calculation, net present value calculation, or comparable transactions.

Valuing an early-stage company is more of an art than a science. There can be no denying the fact that young companies pose the most difficult estimation challenges in valuation. A combination of factors including short and not very informative track record, operating losses and the high probability of failure, all feed into valuation practices that try to avoid dealing with the uncertainty.

By aligning the valuation drivers with the prior steps of the due diligence, we can see that in order of priority, the valuation will tend to be higher when all the following criteria are met:

- The opportunity serves an attractive market with higher growth potential.
- The opportunity has an established competitive position via patents or market share or leadership.
- A strong team is in place.
- The opportunity may demonstrate capital efficiency (needs lower amounts of capital to achieve financial independence).
- A meaningful exit potential within the target time frame can be achieved. In other words, there is a group of strategic buyers that is large, accessible, and seeks growth opportunities via acquisition.
- Finally, the state of the market for capital supply, if excessive it can often elevate valuations across the board.

Early-stage investors can seldom predict whether an opportunity will grow, gain momentum, and generate returns. A classic investment approach is to invest a small amount and gain a seat at the table, i.e. buying an option to invest in future rounds, and if the company begins to grow, investors could maintain or build up their ownership position by investing additional amounts in future rounds.

The discounted cash flow (DCF) method is irrelevant for early-stage ventures on a number of counts. For one, at an early stage of any company, you really don't have a comparable data and the rest is projections. Entrepreneurs usually have a business plan with revenues and expenses projections and they use extensive DCF models to come up with a valuation, but at the end of the day, value is what can be transacted upon.

To calculate valuation of a firm using DCF, we estimate growth rate of revenues and expenses and the number of years of such growth. The entrepreneur's estimates and practitioners' estimates can vary significantly. But let us assume that the two come to some common ground. The second variable is free cash flows (FCF) available during such a period. FCF seems like a novel concept when we discuss startups and early-stage companies. Finally, you have to assume a discount rate and an estimate for the terminal value in order to find Net Present Value (NPV).

The DCF approach is well suited for more mature companies. Startups have little or no revenues, no customers, and at times, operating losses. Even those young companies that are profitable have short histories, and most young firms depend on private capital, initially owner savings. Venture capital and private equity will be drawn upon at a later stage. As a result, many of the standard techniques used to estimate cash flows, growth rates, and discount rates either do not work or yield unrealistic numbers.

In addition, the fact that most young companies do not survive has to be considered somewhere in the valuation. Researchers studied the survival rate of 8.9 million startups worldwide over a seven-year period (2005-2012) and concluded that only 38% of businesses survived over a five-year period (table 3). The survival rate of technology companies (clubbed under Information) is substantially lower than health services, with at least two-thirds of technology companies' shutting down in five years.

The estimated value of a company is based on its future revenues, which in turn implicitly assume that the business will survive. Hence, the possibility of failure needs to be factored in the equation. Furthermore, multiples of valuation should be considered at the point of exit, rather than present-day multiples. If the revenue of a startup after year five were to drop to a compound annual growth rate (CAGR) of 10%, the multiple should reflect this growth as opposed to, say, 50% CAGR in earlier years.

Table 3
Survival Rate of Startups Worldwide

Sector	Year 1	Year 5	Year 7
Health Services	86%	50%	44%
Information	81%	31%	25%
Financial activities	84%	44%	37%
Business Services	82%	38%	31%
All Firms	81%	38%	31%

The basic valuation method of a startup firm looks at the target company at a time in the future when it expects to generate positive cash flows. The future value is then discounted back to the present using a target rate of return (TRR) instead of cost of capital. The TRR is the rate of return that the VC requires when making such a risky investment in a startup. TRR usually ranges between 30% and 80% depending on the perceived risk of the investment.

As an example, consider a venture capitalist who is contemplating a $3 million investment in a company that expects to require no further capital through year 5. The startup company is projected to earn $4 million in year 5 and should be comparable to companies in the sector with a price/earning ratio of 15. The venture capitalist expects to exit the investment through sale of his stock to an acquiring company. Assume further a TRR of 50% on a project of this risk, funded by equity only with no debt.

Required Future Value of the investment = $3(1+0.5)^5$ = $22.8 million

In year 5, the company as a whole will be worth $60 million ($15 \times \$4$ million), based on an assumed comparable P/E multiple of 15 and an expected earnings of $4 million in year 5.

For the VC to receive $22.8 million in year 5 out of $60 million total value of the company, the required ownership at that time must be 38% ($22.8÷$60). The $3 million investment now must give the VC 38% ownership of the startup company. This means the estimate current value of the company is $ 7.9 million.

9.6 Qualities of Successful Entrepreneurs

Successful entrepreneurs share certain traits, which together with a supportive ecosystem allow them to excel. They are not luck lottery winners, but people who have dreams of the future and a well-designed plan to get there.

The Global Entrepreneurship Development Institute (GEDI) introduced an index that measures the quality and dynamics of a country's entrepreneurship ecosystem by taking into account the aspects of the entrepreneurial ecology at the micro and macro levels. It assesses the efficiency of startups' ecosystems and attempts to highlight the bottlenecks that erode the competitive advantages for startups. The Global Entrepreneurship Index (GEI) is a composite of 14 pillars grouped into three sub-indices that are 1- the Entrepreneurial Attitudes Sub-Index, 2- the Entrepreneurial Abilities Sub-Index and 3- the Entrepreneurial Aspirations Sub-Index. A country's score is the simple average of its scores on the three sub-indices, with a higher score reflecting a better ecosystem for entrepreneurship.

The UAE had the highest GEI rank among the Arab countries in 2015 with a global rank of 20, followed by Qatar (24), Saudi Arabia (31), Kuwait (37) and Lebanon (50). Egypt had the lowest rank in the region of 91 globally (chart 3).

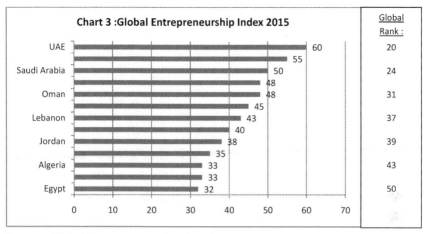

Source: *Global Entrepreneurship Development Institute*

1. Entrepreneurs Work On Their Business, Not In It

While they may have begun building their companies by being involved in every aspect, entrepreneurs understand that in order to lead successful, high-growth businesses, they must dedicate their time and energy to strategic priorities. They excel at focusing on instilling vision and passion, creating great teams, innovating, enhancing brand awareness and partnering with larger corporations to invest in their businesses' infrastructure and technology needs, as well as, sales and regulatory compliance.

2. They Embrace Risk

Entrepreneurs are born with the instinct to go after their goals, irrespective of real or perceived risks. Upon identifying an unmet market need, these entrepreneurs relentlessly set out to solve it.

3. Their Passion Is Infectious

If outstanding entrepreneurs are great at one thing, it is communicating their visions and instilling their passion at all levels of their businesses.

They prioritize building strong teams by investing in the right people, continually upgrading their companies' talents and fostering there teams abilities to anticipate future trends and challenges.

4. They Are Quick To Adapt

Flexibility in the face of challenges is intrinsic to high-growth businesses, making them exceptionally nimble when dealing with obstacles related to changing customer preferences, competitive threats and technological advances. Not only does their ability to rapidly recover from setbacks and adapt to new market situations give them the resilience to weather tough economic conditions, but it also enables them to maintain their momentum, bounce back from bad decisions and learn from their mistakes.

5. They Challenge The Status Quo

Innovation is an ongoing process and part of the corporate culture at successful entrepreneurial companies. Entrepreneurs are willing to secure long-term benefits at the expense of short-term revenues because they understand that constantly innovating their products, services, business models and approaches is key to their survival, growth and market leadership. It also makes them more attractive as investment or acquisition targets for larger corporations.

6. They Seek Innovative Forms Of Financing

Access to finance is a business' lifeline, which is why entrepreneurs who secure a wide range of funding are able to robustly grow their companies. Entrepreneurs place special emphasis on good working capital management and get their funding from a variety of sources, such as angel investments, venture capital, bank loans, private equity, personal funds, friends and family.

Despite their diverging paths to success and the uniqueness of their individual journeys, one common truth remains unchanged: in order for entrepreneurs to thrive, countries must provide them with a supportive ecosystem in terms of tax and regulation, access to funding, education and training, in addition to coordinated support that links them with the public and private sectors, as well as academia.

9.7 The Arab Digital Generation is Underpinning the Entrepreneurial Strength of the Region

A new generation has emerged in the region, those born after the early 1980s, who are extremely active online and the majority of them are consistent users of digital technology. This demographic segment is called the Arab Digital Generation. Although they have similar digital characteristics as other young people around the world, they are distinctly Arab in that they reflect the traditions, challenges and hardships of their region, along with a strong desire to make changes. They are more outspoken about society, economies and politics and have been the force behind the Arab spring. Policy makers, business leaders and financiers are taking note of this dynamic change. But is this new energetic force a political risk or a source of untapped opportunity?

The Arab youth are educated, energetic and possess an entrepreneurial flair. Young people with access to technology are able to take initiative, establish startup ventures and strive to make them successful. They use digital technology to socialize, and with time they browse and shop online for products and services. This will greatly boost demand for innovations, translating into economic and employment benefit for the region.

Although digital technology is driving social and economic shifts worldwide, the MENA region has the potential to embody this more than elsewhere. Here, young people, who have greater adoption rates for new technology, make up a larger portion of the whole population. From 2006 to 2013, the number of Internet users in Arab countries has been growing by 25% annually. By comparison, world Internet users have grown by only 15% annually. As such, the Arab digital generation represents a potentially greater opportunity to innovative products and services than similar groups in other regions.

In the meanwhile, launching startups has become far less expensive than before. Today nearly all the ingredients needed to produce a new website or smartphone application are available online as open source software or cheap pay as-you-go services. Besides, computing power and digital storage are now delivered for free. At Amazon Web Services, the biggest "Cloud" provider, the basic package is free and includes 750 hours of server time. A whole industry of services to help startups improve their offerings has sprung up that will show entrepreneurs how people actually use their products.

On the venture capital side, what is needed are more accomplished investors who can work with entrepreneurs in taking the business from the initial assessment and valuation phase to actual scale and profitability stage. In other words, the gap in round two and round three funding needs to be closed. Once the startups have found the minimum capital required to expand, they must tackle the next hurdle: the region's fragmentation. Each country has its own laws and regulations. E-commerce firms also have to deal with high tariffs, slow border bureaucracies and bad infrastructure.

Governments of the region are called upon to cut red tape, improve education, create competition in telecoms, and legislate supportive legal and regulatory framework and seed accelerators. By putting in place the necessary ecosystem, tech startups will mushroom and the Arab Digital Generation will cease the opportunity to innovate more and create new jobs to this new energetic labor force.

CHAPTER 10

Banking in the Region: Challenges and Opportunities

10.1 Commercial Banking

The regional banking sector was not much affected by the global financial crisis of 2008-2009, and had escaped much of the damage that hit elsewhere. This was due to a mixture of prudent regulation, concentration of activities on domestic assets and liabilities, adequate loan loss reserves and a well capitalized banking sector. According to the Banker magazine's annual survey of the Top 100 Arab banks, their aggregate Tier1 capital reached $250 billion at the end of 2014, an increase of 11% on end of 2012 level. Total assets of banks in the region reached $2,405 billion at end of 2014, with a pre-tax profit of $40 billion and an average return on equity of 16.23%. The banks' average return on assets stood at 1.73% and their average capital adequacy ratio at 10.66%. Total assets of GCC banks ended 2014 at $1,250 billion, accounting for more than 50% of Arab banks' total assets.

Banks in Egypt, Iraq, Lebanon, Morocco and Tunisia have faced challenging operating conditions during the past few years. The ratings of banks in these countries have been negatively impacted by the deteriorating credit worthiness of their respective sovereigns, especially given the concentration of government debt that banks carry on their balance sheet. In Egypt and Lebanon, for example, banks' exposure to government debt stood at 42% and 56% of total assets respectively by the end of 2014. Conflicts or severe internal tensions in neighboring countries (Syria, Libya and Iraq) also had an impact on banking prospects in the other Arab countries where Lebanese, Jordanian and Egyptian banks have branches.

The role that the domestic banks play in supporting the local economy has also increased because of foreign investors' reduced appetite for the region's sovereign debt. For domestic banks, exposure to their respective governments denominated in domestic currency carry attractive yields and zero-risk weighting under Basel regulations. Consequently, domestic government debt represents a multiple of the Egyptian and Lebanese banks' equity base, including more than 10 times the equity base of the large Egyptian public sector banks. This situation effectively exposes banks to critical concentration risks to their respective governments.

In parallel, the profitability, funding and asset quality of banks in these markets have remained fairly resilient despite regional unrest. Asset quality indicators did not deteriorate as banks have tightened their lending standards, and are focusing on existing relationships that they know well, while managing a limited and selective exposure to the retail sector. Non-performing loans could be underestimated, mainly in Egypt and Tunisia, due to the lack of timely identification, recognition and reporting of problem loans. However, banks are expected to have sufficient absorption capacity to manage potential problems that may arise from their credit exposure to the private sector. Deposits will continue to grow, reflecting sustained confidence in banks. Commercial lending opportunities are expected to remain limited for banks in the oil importing Arab countries due to the slow recovery in their domestic economies and to persistent regional political uncertainty.

The most immediate impact of lower oil prices on GCC banks will be felt on the liability side, notably reduced deposit inflows from large government and government-related entities. Direct exposures of banks to GCC governments are limited but, depending on the policy responses, a sustained drop in oil prices could also have pronounced negative effects on public spending, confidence and economic growth. Any immediate impact on asset quality is expected to be low due to the fact that the GCC credit cycle is still in its early stages.

GCC banks could face some funding and liquidity pressures since governments, related entities and National Oil Companies are among the largest depositors in the system, providing around 10% to 35% of banks' non-equity funding. For most of the Gulf banks, market funding is generally limited and liquidity buffers are healthy. GCC banks' liquid assets are equivalent to around 30% of total assets and loan to deposit ratios stand at 90%, on average, leaving some headroom for banks to adjust to changing funding conditions in an orderly fashion.

In its risk assessment of 110 banking systems in advanced and emerging economies Fitch Ratings placed the banking sector of Lebanon, Egypt, Tunisia, Morocco and those of the six GCC countries in the "low level of potential vulnerability" with a score of one, on Fitch's Macro Prudential Indicator (MPI). The MPI tries to identify the build up of potential stress in banking systems due to a specific set of circumstances. It aims to highlight potential systemic stress that could materialize up to three years after an early warning is first indicated. As such, it identifies instances of rapid credit growth over successive two –year periods, along with growth in property prices, an appreciation in the exchange rate or a rise in equity prices. Its assessment is based on three years of annual data, divided into two overlapping two-year periods, with a trigger in either period relevant to a country's MPI score. An MPI score of '1' denotes low potential vulnerability, while a score of '2' reflects moderate vulnerability and a score of '3' denotes a high level of vulnerability to potential systemic stress.

10.2 Implementation of Basel III Requirements for Capital Adequacy

The safety of banks depends on how much capital they hold. Having too little capital in the system may leave it prone to crisis and in need of regular bailouts. Too much capital, on the other hand, could result in huge parts of the banking business becoming unprofitable, leading to higher borrowing costs and slower economic growth. A more pressing danger is that money and risk will flow into the unregulated parts of the economy, possibly making the system even less stable.

The main job of a bank's capital is to absorb losses, acting as a cushion to protect those who have entrusted the bank with their money from adverse market conditions and the mistakes of those who manage the bank. The bank's capital also restrains bankers' instinct for excessive risk taking by raising their leverage ratios beyond what is internationally acceptable. Royal Bank of Scotland, for instance, needed a huge bailout in 2008 not because its losses were so large but because it was excessively leveraged.

Arab banks faired well during the 2008 crisis because they focused on their home markets and leveraged themselves less (the maximum ratio was 20 compared to a leverage ratio of 50 for European and some American banks). Arab banks also relied less on short-term interbank funding and most of them stayed clear from speculative derivative products.

Balance sheets can shrink for other reasons as well. The value of a bank's riskier assets such as mortgages and unsecured loans to companies can drop sharply if the prospects of the borrowers deteriorate. The danger is that the value of the bank's assets could fall below its liabilities leading to the insolvency of the bank. To forestall such failures banks maintain equity. This represents the money a bank's owners have invested in it. Equity takes the first hit when asset values drop. Since the bank's owners absorb the loss, its creditors (bondholders and depositors) can rest assured that they will be bailed out first.

But a bank is not a charity, and the two shock absorbers, cash and liquid assets, are costly. The return on cash is zero, while liquid assets like government bonds yield a low 2%-4%. In contrast, mortgages might generate 7% and unsecured lending closer to 10%. Picking safe and liquid assets lowers returns. In addition equity investors expect a return of around 12% on their shareholding (via dividends or capital gains), compared with the 4% or so demanded by bondholders. This sets up a tension between stability and profitability, which banks must manage. One simple equation explains it:

Return on Equity (RoE) = Return on assets (RoA) x Equity Multiplier

The idea is straightforward. A bank's equity-holders gain when the return on its assets rises. Maximizing RoE means holding fewer safe assets, like cash or government bonds, since these provide low returns. When return on all asset classes fall, as in the early 2000s, banks have another way to boost RoE: leverage (equity multiplier is defined as the ratio of bank's assets to its equity). Banks can increase their leverage by borrowing more from depositors or debt markets and lending or investing the proceeds. That gives them more income-generating assets relative to the same pool of equity.

Under the original international capital accord struck in Basel in 1988, banks were meant to hold capital worth 8% of their assets. Since certain assets are safer than others, and some banks are better at lending safely than others, it seemed sensible to allow banks to calculate how much capital they actually needed, gauged by the probability of their own loans defaulting. Basel II, a revised set of rules introduced risk-weighted assets. Banks with the creditworthy clients could hold the least capital whereas those who pursued riskier business had to hold more. A summery of the risk-based capital is given below:

Basel II: Summery of the Risk-Based Capital Standards for On-Balance-Sheet Items

Risk Categories

Category 1(0% weight): Cash, reserve balances at the Central bank, securities of the U.S. Treasury, OECD governments and local government bonds issued in the respective domestic currency. Loans to sovereigns with an S&P credit rating of AA – or better.

Category 2(20% weight): Cash items in the process of collection. U.S. and OECD interbank deposits and guaranteed claims. Some non-OECD banks and government deposits securities and General obligation municipal bonds. Loans to sovereigns with an S&P credit rating of A+ to A-. Loans to banks and corporates with an S&P credit rating of AA- or better.

Category 3(50% weight): Loans fully secured by residential properties. Loans to corporates with an S&P credit rating of BBB+ to BBB-. Loans to sovereigns with an S&P credit rating of A+ to A-.

Category 4(100% weight): Loans to sovereigns with an S&P credit rating of BB+ to B-. Loans to banks with a credit rating of BBB+ to B-. Loans to corporates with a credit rating of BBB+ to BB-. All other on-balance sheet assets not listed above, including loans to private entities and individuals, some claims on non-OECD governments and banks, real assets, and investments in subsidiaries.

Category 5 (150% weight): Loans to sovereigns, banks, and securities firms with an S&P credit rating below B-. Loans to corporates with credit rating below BB-.

The new rules on capital, known as Basel III, force banks to hold a lot more capital and by requiring much of it to be in equity. In essence, they will more than triple the amount of equity that most large banks will have to hold compared with the period before the crisis. Banks will be required to hold a capital conservation buffer of 2.5% on top of tier 1 capital that can be used to absorb losses during periods of stress. Minimum capital will therefore rise from 8% to 10.5% by 2019, but many Arab banks are getting there early to show they are ready. The increase is much larger than it appears because under the new rules banks must hold at least 7% in equity. These rules have also closed loopholes that allowed banks to hold less capital, for instance by shifting assets off their balance sheets or classifying them as trading assets.

The liquidity coverage and net stable funding requirements that were introduced as part of the Basel III capital framework would be credit positive for banks in the region. The new requirements stipulate that banks should hold higher balances of more-liquid assets and should fund less liquid assets with more stable funding, in order to be prepared to face one-off or market-based liquidity shocks. As such, banks will try to minimize their reliance on uninsured financial liabilities, such as inter-bank and short-term money market sources, and will be enhancing the stability and duration of their funding to better match long term and less liquid assets such as loans.

However, the emphasis on funding stability and asset liquidity could hurt banks' profitability as a result of holding lower yielding liquid assets and extending out funding maturity profiles. Higher funding costs and lower asset yields would erode profitability if banks cannot compensate by re-pricing products or cutting costs. It is anticipated that the banks' returns on investment portfolios to decline because of the need to hold more qualifying high quality liquid assets with lower yields.

The massive increase in capital envisaged should show convincingly that the system itself is better buffered against loss. This will involve huge sums of money. Standard & Poor's, a rating agency, looked at 75 of the world's biggest banks and found that between them they will have to raise $763 billion in equity by 2019 just to meet the new minimum. If smaller institutions are included, European banks will need to come up with $1.3 trillion in equity by 2019 and American banks will have to raise $870 billion, and Arab banks $20 billion.

Many countries are now also considering getting banks to hold an additional cushion of convertible capital. Convertible capital instruments, usually known as contingent convertible bonds or Cocos, are bonds that turn into equity if the bank's capital ratio falls too low.

10.3 Credit Conditions in the region

The role of governments in the region's credit markets is quite visible. On average the ratio of bank credit to government and state owned enterprises to GDP is close to 18%, compared to world's average of 6.8%. Bank credit to GDP is higher than deposit to GDP for most Arab countries, suggesting that countries of the region provide credit at a faster pace than their ability to raise deposits. This means greater reliance in certain countries on non- deposit or wholesale sources of funds (including cross- border interbank funding) (table 1).

Table 1
Credit and Banking Conditions, MENA vs. World, 2007-2012

Country	Credit to Govt. Firms to GDP	Bank Deposits to GDP	Bank private Credit to GDP	Bank Credit to Bank Deposits	Liquid assets to Deposits and Short-term Funding	NPLs to Gross Loans	Provisions to NPLs	Lending-Deposit Spread	Net Interest Margin
Egypt	33.1	69.7	37.0	51.9	43.6	14.4	90.7	5.3	2.2
Jordan	29.9	95.8	75.3	77.6	36.3	6.3	58.4	4.4	3.3
Lebanon	69.3	206.2	67.9	32.7	34.8	6.3	60.8	2.1	2.3
Mauritania	5.9	20.2	24.3	118.6	48.5	...	...	11.5	3.7
Morocco	17.2	82.7	69.0	84.1	28.5	5.7	72.7	...	3.0
Sudan	3.6	12.5	10.1	77.6	55.4	...	...	...	3.9
Syrian Arab Republic	24.0	45.7	16.6	37.1	60.7	...	...	2.8	2.9
Tunisia	5.0	48.3	57.9	120.8	24.0	...	...	...	3.2
Average (oil importing countries)	**23.5**	**72.6**	**44.8**	**75.1**	**41.5**	**8.2**	**70.6**	**5.2**	**3.0**
Bahrain	14.8	68.0	61.7	91.6	30.4	...	...	5.7	2.1
Kuwait	5.3	59.2	61.4	103.6	25.2	7.8	37.1	3.0	3.0
Oman	4.5	31.6	36.6	116.5	27.8	2.7	113.4	3.2	3.6
Qatar	25.8	46.5	39.2	84.7	29.1	...	...	3.6	2.9
Saudi Arabia	12.3	51.6	41.5	80.4	16.4	2.5	125.4	...	3.1
United Arab Emirates	16.2	61.1	67.5	108.5	23.4	4.2	...	...	2.8
GCC Average	**13.2**	**48.4**	**51.3**	**112.4**	**25.4**	**4.3**	**92.0**	**3.9**	**2.9**
MENA Average	17.6	54.4	38.7	76.9	41.7	6.2	79.8	4.7	3.4
World	6.8	41.5	36.0	85.3	32.1	3.6	65.6	6.3	4.2

Source: Global Financial Development Database, World Bank, April 2014,
except for Bank credit to bank deposits for Saudi Arabia (from the IFS).

On average the share of liquid assets to deposits and short term funding is highest in the MENA region (close to 42%) exceeding a world's average of 32%. This may reflect reserves of high quality liquid assets at the Central Banks, an indirect way of funding the government. This has an opportunity cost of less lending to the private sectors.

The quality of the loan portfolio in the oil importing Arab countries is worse than the world average. The ratio of non-performing loans (NPLs) to total loans stood at an average of 8.2% versus 3.6% for the world. Provisioning is generally in line with world figures, but the lending-deposit spread is lower than the world average (5.2% versus 6.3%). High NPLs and low spreads in the region's oil importing countries may be indicative of underpricing of loans, suggesting that credit risk management practices could be lagging.

In the GCC countries, the lending-deposit spread is narrower (3.9%), and it is low in Jordan and Lebanon as well, supported by direct debiting of government salaries and higher exposure to autonomous government bodies. The relatively lower risk involved may justify a lower interest spread. Low credit spreads over deposits for GCC countries also result in narrower interest rate margin, on average 2.9%. The phenomena of salary assignment, whereby a customer assigns his salary to a bank in order to access loan facilities, has evolved as a means of reducing credit risk in the retail banking sector not only in the Gulf countries but also in Jordan, Lebanon and Egypt.

Focusing on the levels and patterns of Loan-to-Deposit (LTD) ratios across the MENA region reveals some striking differences (table 2). Generally LTD ratios range between 60% and 90%, compared to a world average of 85%. Values below 60% are considered markedly low and those above 90% are considered excessively high. LTD ratios for Lebanon, Egypt and Syria fall below 50%. This can be explained by a combination of relatively weak loan demand and high government borrowing requirements financed domestically. On the other end, most GCC banks exhibit high LTD ratios, implying greater reliance on large wholesale funding, including cross-border which is deemed to be less stable source of financing.

Table 2
Evolution of Loan-to-Deposit Ratios in MENA, (2008-2013)

Country	2008	2009	2010	2011	2012	2013	2008-2013
Egypt	56.4	55.5	53.1	50.7	49.5	48.9	52.4
Jordan	84.0	85.1	78.0	74.5	74.7	74.9	78.5
Lebanon	31.6	33.4	32.6	34.6	37.2	38.8	34.7
Mauritania	134.4	136.7	142.6	134.5	121.1	115.2	130.7
Morocco	65.0	70.9	73.8	76.4	79.9	81.1	74.5
Sudan	82.1	79.2	76.4	71.8	67.6	63.6	73.4
Syrian Arab Republic	32.6	33.6	36.0	39.8	44.4	...	37.3
Tunisia	119.4	115.5	115.9	120.2	129.7	131.5	122.0
Average (oil importing Countries)	75.7	76.2	76.1	75.3	75.5	79.1	75.5
Bahrain	81.9	90.1	94.5	89.0	95.2	99.8	91.8
Kuwait	100.7	106.1	98.1	99.1	97.1	97.0	99.7
Oman	102.3	113.7	121.2	121.0	121.8	123.5	117.3
Qatar	83.0	86.1	97.1	80.9	77.3	73.8	82.4
Saudi Arabia	79.6	86.3	79.7	79.3	77.0	79.2	80.2
United Arab Emirates	98.2	110.6	115.8	108.3	102.3	102.4	106.3
GCC Average	93.4	101.2	103.0	98.4	97.0	97.9	96.3
MENA Average	71.3	74.0	74.4	72.6	72.0	73.6	71.6

Source: Based on data from the International Financial Statistics

Recent analysis suggests greater lending by global banks to GCC countries compared to pre 2008 crisis peaks, as well as, an increase in funding through bond and Sukuk issuance. Also increasingly more deposits came from governments and quazi government institutions during this period of high oil prices.

Real growth rate in credit and deposits have accelerated in the last few years in Kuwait, Oman, and Saudi Arabia, with Iraq and Qatar exhibiting the highest growth rates in the region. On the other hand, in most oil importing countries (Jordan, Lebanon, Morocco, Syria, and Tunisia), real credit growth has generally decelerated since 2009.

10.4 The Rising Importance of Peer-to-Peer Lending

Whereas a bank intermediates between savers and borrowers by entering into separate transactions with them, taking all the risk that such transactions entail, peer-to-peer lending (P2P) is merely a matchmaker between savers and borrowers through some sort of online system. Lenders earn a higher rate of interest than they can get on a bank deposit, while borrowers pay less than they would on a loan from a bank if such loans were at all available to them. The P2P Company makes money by levying a fee, usually a small percentage of the money lent, to both borrowers and lenders but does not take any risks itself. If borrowers do not repay their loans, those who advanced them money will carry all the risk. Unlike bank depositors there is no government guarantee, and unlike bank loans, there is no collateral to secure the loans.

The scale of P2P lending worldwide is still modest. The two biggest American outfits, Lending Club and Prosper, have lent only $8 billion between them in 2014, a small share of American's personal loan market of $1,800 billion. But the rate of growth is huge; their lending has grown by 3,000% in eight years (2006-2014).

Doing banking without the expensive bits of industry-branches, IT systems, head offices, and so on, means that peer-to-peer loans offer lower rates, reflecting their reduced costs. Most borrowers are refinancing their credit-card debt, swapping a loan on which they paid 16-18% for 10% or so at Lending Club. The company's focus has been on smaller loans (up to $35,000) to individuals with decent credit ratings, although it has also started catering to businesses recently.

Peer-to-peer lenders use credit scores as a starting-point to establish a borrower's creditworthiness in the same way as banks and credit-card companies do. But they claim their credit-scoring algorithms and their creative use of data derived from social media will enable them to weed out probable defaulters better than conventional financial firms do, leading to smaller losses (best not to tweet about walking away from your electricity bill).

The small scale of P2P lending suggests enormous room for growth. Borrowers are pleased to have a new financing option that does not call for a collateral. Investors can choose which loans to underwrite; others opt to participate in a bundle of loans to reduce risk of default. Over time this new opportunity has the potential to take the consumer lending business from banks and credit card sellers, in the same way taxi companies has been disturbed by Uber.

The opportunity for P2P lending in the MENA region is even more pronounced than in other geographies. Bank lending to consumers, students and SMEs is more limited than in OECD countries. Without collateral or salary assignment it will be very difficult to extend loans to meet the operational needs of small businesses or to finance consumer expenditures. The percentage of SME loans to total loans in the MENA region varies from a low of 0.5% in Qatar to 5% in Egypt and 24% in Morocco (chart 1). It is estimated that a funding gap of $25 billion currently exists in the region. Liwwa is a newly established P2P company that has started operations in the MENA Region in 2015.

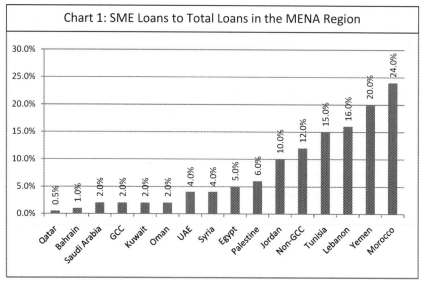

Source: OECD 2015

10.5 Investment Banking in the Region

The investment banking activities in the MENA region comprises equity capital markets, debt capital markets, brokerage, wealth management, fund and asset management and equity research. The region's investment banking market was strong between 2004-2007, averaging 17% annual growth. After peaking at $7 billion in 2007, the region's investment banking market began to shrink. The financial crisis of 2008-2009 saw investment banking activities dropping by 25% before stabilizing in 2010 and since then it has been on a slow upward trend.

While commercial banks in the region remained generally profitable during the global financial crisis and the uprisings that took place in several Arab spring countries in 2011-2012, the region's leading investment banks experienced tough times. Global Investment House of Kuwait, Shuaa Capital of Dubai, EFG Hermes of Egypt, National Investor of Abu Dhabi, Gulf Finance House in Bahrain among others all suffered major declines and few of them came close to shutting down.

The retrenchment of the local and regional investment banks (IBs) allowed the international investment banks with regional head offices in Dubai, Bahrain or Riyadh to dominate the league tables. Smaller debt and equity issues of $20 million to $100 million, the bread and butter of the local and regional IBs dried up completely, while issues exceeding $100 million, from government and large corporates all went to the international IBs.

The sharp drop in investment banking revenues for the period 2008-2012 was due to the decline of trading volumes in the region's stock exchanges, with brokerage fees dropping to a fraction of their previous levels. Primary capital markets (IPOs, secondary offerings, debt issuance) were virtually closed. Mergers and acquisitions deals became scarce, assets under management shrunk in value while mark to market losses on the IB's illiquid investments surged.

The period 2013-2014 saw an upturn in the region's investment banking activities. New issuance of bonds and Sukuk recorded an annual increase of 15%, with total value reaching $46.1 billion by the end of 2013 and $50 billion by the end of 2014. Completed mergers and acquisitions (M&As) deals reached $50 billion in 2014. The majority of the growth was due to the increase in activity of UAE and Saudi based corporates.

From a geographic perspective, deal activity remains driven by a strong performance in the GCC countries coupled with an ongoing pick-up in selected Arab Spring countries like Egypt and Morocco. The GCC accounts for the bulk of the M&As deals, with 44% and 43% respectively of the announced value and volume of completed deals during 2014. This is compared to 69% and 43% respectively during 2013, in an indication of larger deals being closed outside GCC.

Foreign acquirers have been one major component of the M&A deals in the MENA region. During 2014, they have accounted for 54% of the number of completed deals, compared to 51% during 2013, slightly below the average of 57% witnessed during 2009 and 2010. These numbers reflect a confidence of global players in a large number of regional economies and their long-term fundamentals. In return, it offers some interesting exit options for local investors.

The MENA IPO market surged as well in 2013-2014, with 27 IPOs raising $11.5 billion in 2014 on top of the 24 IPOs that raised $3.5 billion in 2013. The UAE and Saudi Arabia led the MENA region with total IPO proceeds of about $10 billion in 2014.

After decades during which Arab banks rarely ventured outside their region, they are starting to play major roles in arranging bonds and Sukuk deals overseas, competing with long-established international banks. This is partly because Arab banks have gained depth and sophistication in their domestic markets, allowing them to build up their technical expertise in structuring and placing of fixed income securities. But it is also because the global financial crisis has made the Gulf more attractive to overseas bond and Sukuk issuers as a source of investment funds. Gulf banks are seen as the best channels for issuers to attract money.

The trend is still in its infancy. In lists of the top 25 arrangers of bond issues globally by monetary value in 2014, no Arab bank appears. Even in their home markets, Arab banks are still not dominant. Among the 25 most active arrangers of international bonds from Arab issuers in 2014, the highest-ranked institution was National Bank of Abu Dhabi (NBAD) in sixth place, and Emirates NBD of Dubai in the seventh place. Only 10 of 25 banks were from the region, the list featured a wide range of banks from Europe and the United States and Asia, and was headed by HSBC.

However, the last several years have seen a big change. As recently as 2011, the top 25 arrangers did not include any Arab bank at all. Now, even relatively small institutions such as Dubai Islamic Bank and Qatar's Barwa Bank have entered the league tables.

There is evidence that the entry of Arab banks into the bond arranging business within their region has increased competition and squeezed fees, making it more attractive for the Arab institutions to seek arranging activity outside their region. According to estimates by Thomson Reuters, fees for international dollar bonds arranged in the region in 2014 have totaled about 0.22% of the size of deals, down from roughly 0.58% in 2010.

The global financial crisis supported the trend, by forcing many Western banks to downsize their operations in the MENA region as they focused on repairing balance sheets back home. Similarly, the introduction of tighter global capital rules in Basel III over the next few years may help Arab banks, many of them are flush with capital, while many Western banks may need to retrench.

In fact, Sukuk are emerging as a key area in which Gulf banks can expand internationally. Although several foreign banks have major expertise in Sukuk, the Gulf banks are based in countries where Islamic banking is mainstream, and some are dedicated Islamic banks themselves, this may give them an advantage in developing their Sukuk arranging capabilities. When Britain raised £200 million ($345 million) through five-year Sukuk in June 2014, two of the five banks mandated to arrange the issue were from the Gulf: National Bank of Abu Dhabi and Qatar's Barwa Bank. They worked along side HSBC, Standard Chartered and Malaysia's CIMB.

Arab banks are well suited to handle the investment banking activities of the region owing to their huge balance sheets and large customer base. However, the results of such activities have so far been mixed. Historically, commercial banks perceived capital market activities to compete with their core lending business, and most of the time, they were unlikely to encourage their clients to issue public debt in lieu of syndicated loans. Banks have maintained a credit mindset, and were not geared to adequately underwrite equity issues. However, the more progressive of them have established subsidiaries such as Al-Rajhi Capital, NCB Capital, NBK Capital, and QNB Capital, to provide investment-banking services to their clients.

10.6 Future outlook: The Challenge Ahead

Going forward, funding for investment firms in the region will become more of a challenge. The business model of universal banking is expected to take hold where the region's commercial banks will either acquire investment firms, or as many have already done, establish their own investment banking units. Those who want to maintain their autonomy as investment banks may choose to merge with another IB in the region or raise more equity.

The region's IBs do not have many options to draw upon. The easiest way would be through discounted offerings such as rights issues or selling assets at fire sale prices. Although the debt to equity ratio of the regional investment banking institutions tend to be in the single digit, compared to more than 20 for the global investment banks, nevertheless additional equity would give the regional firms the ammunition needed to ride any future down cycle.

Commercial banks are expected to become more involved in investment banking while seeking to de-risk their balance sheet, and increase their fee income. They are definitely capable of underwriting large issues, and are well poised to effectively place them given their distribution capabilities.

The larger regional transactions (especially involving energy companies, and telecommunications) have so far, been dominated by international investment banks. The middle-market and smaller deals are competed upon by the big-four audit firms (PwC, EY, KPMG, Deloitte) and a large number of local investment banks. The local IBs are likely to continue to focus on country transactions that dominate deal flow for middle-market and will start to selectively compete with the international IBs for the large deals.

While few full fledged regional investment banks are likely to surface, offering advisory, capital raising (debt & equity), asset and wealth management and trading, most of the sector will be dominated by specialized investment banking firms concentrating on one aspect of the business, e.g. issuance of Sukuk, regional asset management, Islamic funds, local stock market funds, M&As, etc.

Investment banking relies on expensive talent to succeed. It is important therefore to develop local expertise and offer them attractive remunerations and incentive schemes to retain their services. The national talent is proving to be essential to any investment bank, especially for access to transactions, knowledge of the local regulatory and legal landscape, understanding the stakeholders, and appreciation of the local business values.

The well-established investment banking in the region, which does not have a solvency problem, should be allowed to become deposit taking institutions, and put under the supervision and scrutiny of the central banks, in line with similar developments globally. This will give these firms access to wholesale sources of deposits from corporates and public sector institutions and they will be able to draw, when needed, on the liquidity and discount facilities of their respective monetary authority. Those benefitting from such a privilege should be forced to adhere to strict conditions of liquidity, debt to equity ratio and ownership of non-financial assets.

The government of Kuwait unveiled a plan that requires investment firms operating in the country who benefit from loans backed by state guarantees to enter in a merger with one or several other such firms. Governments of the region are called upon to become more "interventionist" towards their banking and financial sectors. For example, they could take illiquid or hard to trade assets off the balance sheet of the investment firms in return for treasury bills and bonds. Governments could also choose to inject equity in these firms. Hopefully this will provide enough incentives for the stronger commercial banks to acquire some of the troubled investment banking firms.

CHAPTER 11

Managing Risk in the Region's Financial Markets

11.1 Introduction: The Need for a Risk Plan

Financial Institutions must take risks if they are to survive and prosper. The primary responsibility of risk management is to understand the risks that the institution is currently taking and the risks it plans to take in the future. It must decide whether the risks are acceptable and, if they are not, what action should be taken. Huge "subprime" losses at Lehman Brothers and Merrill Lynch would have been less severe if the risk management department had been able to convince senior management that unacceptable risks were being taken and the right hedging mechanism was not put in place.

Many natural phenomena, such as people's heights, conform to what is known as the normal distribution or the "bell curve". If the average male height is around 178cm, the number of men who are shorter or taller will decline the further you get from that average. The normal distribution is easy to model: 95% of the data will be within two standard deviations of the mean. It is thus common to use the normal distribution when calculating, for example, the "value at risk" of a portfolio. But financial markets tend to have "fat tails" –more extreme outcomes, in the form of bubbles and crashes, than the normal distribution would suggest. The 23% fall in the Dow Jones Industrial Average on October 19th 1987 is an obvious example. Markets tend to rise more slowly than they fall. They may take months to advance by 15-20% but can drop that far in a week or even a day.

The concept of a free-risk asset is quite useful in finance. It provides the base from which other assets can be priced. Corporate borrowers pay an interest premium over the risk-free rate, equities have offered a higher long-term return than government bonds to reflect their higher risk. But what is the risk-free rate? Multinational companies can borrow at a lower rate of interest than some governments (e.g. Apple compared to Greece). Although the USA is the world's biggest economy, its government does not borrow at the cheapest rate in the world. Japanese and German yields have been for many years lower than those of the US.

Where America does have a substantial advantage is that it borrows in the world's reserve currency (the dollar) and that its debt market is by far the most liquid. The result is that Treasury bills, in particular, play a vital role in the system as cash equivalents and as collateral for short-term loans and derivative contracts. US treasury bills are seen as risk- free in this context in that they are instantly and universally acceptable to all participants in the system. They are the oil that lubricates the global machinery of finance.

A government with debt denominated in its own currency would not default, because it simply prints more money to pay off the debt. In practice, however, countries do default on local-currency debt: six have done so in the past 15 years, including Jamaica, Russia and Ecuador. From the point of view of a creditor, however, the ability of a government to print money is of little comfort if the result is higher inflation (for domestic investors) or currency depreciation (for foreign ones).

Businesses should not only have a strategy plan but a risk plan as well. This includes a detailed analysis of various risks and ways and means to manage them. Traditionally, a number of companies worked on the model of decomposing different risks and aligning the risk management function into silos such as credit risk, market risk, operational risk etc. However, key risk indicators coming out of various departments may have lacked coherence or perhaps had given conflicting messages to the decision makers. Different risks that a firm is exposed to are interdependent and should be viewed as a business-wide activity impacting everything that the business is engaged in.

Both key performance indicators (KPIs) and key risk indicators (KRIs) work in tandem. KRIs help the company avoid problems so that KPIs achieve good performance. KRIs are forward looking and serve an early alarm bell for a potential risk to the business. In contrast, KPIs are tools employed to measure past performance. When KRIs are integrated with business strategies, the task of identifying, evaluating and understanding potential risks to the business becomes easier. This in turn aids the board and senior management to take timely and adequate measures to avoid potential hazards.

11.2 How Risks are Managed

An effective overall corporate strategy combines a set of activities that a financial institution plans to undertake with an adequate assessment of the risks included in these activities. Unfortunately, many banks have forgotten the second part of that definition. In other words, there can be no real strategic management in financial services without risk management.

Risk management needs to be combined into all aspects of the firm's business and should be part of the calculus for all decision-making. Strategic decisions about what activities to undertake should not be made unless senior management understands the risks involved. Assessing potential returns without fully analyzing the corresponding risks to the organization would be incomplete, and potentially harmful, analysis. Building a rigorous strategic risk management framework requires the institution to examine both its internal practices and its external environment, and to understand how closely the two are connected.

There are two broad risk management strategies open to an Arab financial institution. One approach is to identify risks one by one and handle each one separately. This is sometimes referred to as risk decomposition. The other is to reduce risk by being well diversified. This is sometimes referred to as risk aggregation. Financial institutions typically use both approaches.

Consider, for example, the market risks incurred by the trading room of an Arab financial institution. These risks depend on the future movements in a multiple of market variables (exchange rates, interest rates, stock prices, and so on). To implement the risk decomposition approach, the trading room is organized so that a trader is responsible for trades related to just one market variable (or perhaps a small group of market variables). For example, there could be one trader who is responsible for all trades involving the Saudi riyal-yen exchange rate. At the end of each day, the trader is required to insure that certain risk measures are kept within limits specified by the management. If by the end of the day it looks as though one or more of the risk measures will be outside the specified limits, the trader must either get special permission to maintain the position or execute new hedging trades so that the limits are adhered to.

The risk managers, working in what is termed the "middle office" of a bank, implement the risk aggregation approach for the market risk being taken. This involves calculating at the end of each day the total risk faced by the bank from movements in all market variables. Hopefully, the bank is well diversified so that its overall exposure to market movement is fairly small. If risks are unacceptably high, then the reasons must be determined and the necessary corrective action is taken.

Credit risks are traditionally managed using risk aggregation. It is important for financial institutions to be well diversified. If, for example, a bank lends 40% of its available funds to a single borrower, it is not well diversified and likely to be subject to unacceptable risks. If the borrower runs into financial difficulties and is unable to make interest and principle payments, the bank could become insolvent. If the bank adopts a more diversified strategy of lending 1% of its available funds to each of 1000 different borrowers, it would then be in much safer position. Suppose that in an average year the probability of any one-borrower defaulting is 1%. We can expect that close to 10 borrowers will default in the year and the losses on these borrowers will be more than offset by the profits earned on the 99% of loans that perform well. To maximize the benefits of diversification, borrowers should be in different geographical regions and in different industries.

Value at risk (VaR) provides a single number that summarizes the total risk of a bank or a corporation. In essence, it asks the simple question "How bad can things get"? The variable V is the value at risk of a company. It is a function of two parameters: the time horizon T and the confidence level, X%. VaR is the loss level during a time period of length T that we are X% certain will not be exceeded. If T is five days and X is 95, the company is 95% certain that it will not lose more than V over the next 5 days.

Consider, for instance, an Egyptian Bank that holds a $10 million foreign exchange position. How much could the bank possibly lose over a one-day holding period with a 99% level of confidence? The first step for the calculation of VaR is to determine the bank's exposure to the foreign exchange market risk, i.e. the foreign exchange position in Egyptian pound. The next step is estimate the variability of the risk factor using standard deviation of returns of EP/USD exchange rate. Suppose that the returns are normally distributed with a weekly volatility (standard deviation) of 0.408% and that the exchange rate at the time of calculating VaR is 8 EP/USD. It follows that VaR with a confidence level of 99% and for a one week holding period is EP 838,848. The 99% corresponds to the 0.495% or half the total area under the standard normal distribution (profit and loss distribution), with the corresponding Z=2.57.

VaR = Total exposure x daily Volatility x 0.495 quartile of normal distribution
VaR = (8 x 10,000,000) x (0.408% x 2.57) = EP 838,848

In other words there is 99% chance that losses will not exceed EP 838,848 for a one-week holding of the $10 million foreign exchange position.

11.3 Risk Versus Return for Investors

There is a trade-off between risk and return when money is invested. The greater the risks taken, the higher is the realized return. The trade-off is actually between risk and expected return, not between risk and actual return. The term "expected return" sometimes causes confusion. In everyday language an outcome that is "expected" is considered highly likely to occur. However, statisticians define the expected value of a variable as its average or (mean) value. Expected return is therefore a weighted average of the possible returns, where the weight applied to a particular return equals the probability of that return occurring. The possible returns and their probabilities can be either estimated from historical data or assessed subjectively.

Suppose, for example, that you have $100,000 to invest for one year. One alternative is to buy Treasury bills yielding 5% per annum. There is then no risk and the expected return is 5%. Another alternative is to invest the $ 100,000 in equities (S&P 500 stock market index). To simplify things, we suppose that the possible outcomes from those investments are as shown in Table 1. There is a 0.05 probability that the return will be +50%, there is a 0.25 probability that the return will be +30%, and so on. Expressing the returns in decimal form, the expected return per year is:

(0.05x0.50) + (0.25x0.30) + (0.40x0.10) + 0.25 x (-0.10) + 0.05 x (-0.30) = 0.10

This shows that in return for taking some risk you are able to increase your expected return per annum from the 5% offered by Treasury bills to 10% return if invested in a stock. If things work out well, your return per annum could be as high as 50%. But the worst-case outcome is a -30% return or a loss of $30,000.

Table 1 Return in One Year from Investing $100,000 in Equities: US's stock market index S&P 500.

Probability	Return
0.05	+50%
0.25	+30%
0.40	+10%
0.25	-10%
0.05	-30%

11.4 Credit Ratings

Credit ratings provide information that is widely used by financial market participants for the management of credit risks. A credit rating is a measure of the credit quality of a debt instrument such as a bond or a loan. However, the rating of a corporate or sovereign bond is often assumed to be an attribute of the bond issuer rather than of the bond itself. Thus, if the bonds issued by a country or company has a rating of AAA, the country or the company is often referred to as having a rating of AAA.

The three major credit rating agencies are Moody's, S&P, and Fitch. The best ratings assigned by S&P and by Moody's are AAA and Aaa respectively. Bonds with this rating are considered to have minimal chance of defaulting. The next best rating is AA for S&P and Aa for Moody's. Following that we have: A, Baa, Ba, B, Caa, Ca, and C for Moody's. The S&P ratings corresponding to Moody's are, A, BBB, BB, B, CCC, CC, and C, respectively. To create finer rating measures S&P divides its AA rating category into AA+, AA, and AA-, it divides it's A rating category into A+, A, and A-, and so on. Moody's Aaa rating category and S&P's AAA rating are not subdivided, nor usually are the two lowest rating categories. Fitch's rating categories are similar to those of S&P.

The ratings assigned by different agencies are assumed to be equivalent. For example, a BBB+ rating from S&P is considered equivalent to a Baa1 rating from Moody's. Instruments with ratings of BBB- (Baa3) or above are considered to be investment grade. Those with ratings below BBB- (Baa3) are termed noninvestment grade or speculative grade or junk bonds.

Table 2 gives the credit ratings of the various Arab countries together with other basic macro risk variables.

Table 2
Risk Matrices For Arab Countries: 2014

Ratings			Public Debt/ GDP (%)	Debt Service Ratio (%)
	S&P	Moody's		
Kuwait	AA (stable)	Aa 2 (negative)	6.5	7.2
Qatar	AA (stable)	AA2 (stable)	32.0	12.7
UAE	AA- (stable)		32.1	3.9
Saudi Arabia	AA- (negative)	Aa3 (stable)	3.7	1.8
Oman	A- (stable)	A1 (stable)	4.0	3.6
Bahrain	BBB- (negative)	Baa2 (negative)	39.9	15.3
Jordan	BB- (negative)	B1 (negative)	83.9	10.2
Egypt	B- (stable)	Caa1 (negative)	97.5	4.7
Lebanon	B- (negative)	B1 (negative)	143.9	21.0
Tunisia	BB- (negative)	Ba3 (negative)	47.4	9.8
Morocco	BBB- (negative)	Ba1 (negative)	62.0	6.9
Iraq	CCC (stable)	_	41.0	Not available

Source: IMF, World Economic Outlook, 2015

11.5 Various Risks Faced by Financial Institutions in the Region.

As mentioned before, a major objective of management of Arab Financial institutions is to maximize return on equity to the firm's shareholders. However, this often comes at the cost of increased risk. The various risks facing a financial institution include: credit risk, liquidity risk, interest rate risk, market risk, off-balance sheet risk, foreign exchange risk, country or sovereign risk, technology risk, operational risk and insolvency risk. Table 3 presents a brief definition of each of these risks. The effective management of these risks is central to the performance of the financial institution. It can be argued that the main business of financial institutions is to manage these risks.

Table 3
Risks Faced by Financial Institutions

1. **Credit Risk-** the risk that promised cash flows from loans and securities held by financial institutions may not be paid in full or on time.
2. **Liquidity Risk-** the risk that a sudden and unexpected increase in liability withdrawals may require a financial institution to liquidate assets in a very short period of time and at low prices.
3. **Interest Rate Risk-** the risk incurred by a financial institution when the maturities of its assets and liabilities are mismatched and interest rates are volatile.
4. **Market Risk-** the risk incurred in trading assets and liabilities due to changes in interest rates, exchange rates, share prices and other asset prices.
5. **Off-Balance-Sheet Risk-** the risk incurred by a financial institution as the result of its activities related to contingent assets and liabilities.

6. **Foreign Exchange Risk-** the risk that exchange rate changes can affect the value of a financial institution's assets and liabilities denominated in foreign currencies.
7. **Country or Sovereign Risk-** the risk that repayments by foreign borrowers may be interrupted because of interference from foreign governments or other political entities.
8. **Technology Risk-** the risk incurred by a financial institution when its technological investment does not produce anticipated cost savings.
9. **Operational Risk-** the risk that existing technology or support systems may malfunction, that fraud may occur that impacts the activities of the financial institution and/or external shocks such as hurricanes and floods occur.
10. **Insolvency Risk-** the risk that a financial institution may not have enough capital to offset a sudden decline in the value of its assets relative to its liabilities.

1. Credit Risk

Credit risk arises because of the possibility that promised cash flows on financial claims held by financial institutions (FIs), such as loans, bonds or Sukuk will not be paid in full. FIs that buy bonds and Sukuk of long maturities are more exposed than are FIs that buy shorter maturities. The key role of FIs involves screening and monitoring loans and bonds to insure that only the credit worthy issues will be invested in. This means there is a high probability that the borrower/issuer will pay interest and principle on time, and a low probability of a downside risk of default. In the event of default, the FI earns zero interest on the asset or fee on the bonds or Sukuk and may well lose all or part of the principle depending on the ability of the FI to lay claim to some of the borrower's collateral backing these issues.

One of the advantages that FIs have over individual investors is their ability to diversify credit risk exposures by exploiting the law of large numbers in their asset investment portfolios. Diversification across borrowers, assets (loans, bonds, Sukuk), and by maturities reduces the overall credit risk in the asset portfolio and thus increases the probability of partial or full repayment of principal and/or interest. In particular, diversification reduces individual firm-specific credit risks, while still leaving the FI exposed to systematic credit risk, such as factors that simultaneously increase the default risk of all firms in the economy (e.g. economic recession, war, or sudden market collapse).

An important element in the credit management process is pricing, or risk based profitability, where the interest rates or fees charged are commensurate with the riskiness of the borrower. Another element is buying insurance against default (credit default swaps), a third element is screening issuers/borrowers based on their credit history to insure that the FI only funds the most credit worthy loans, and a fourth element is having the necessary collateral that can be sold in case of default. Bank lending is normally capped at 50% of market value of the collateral. Finally, the FI should adhere to a policy of diversification by sector and borrower, limiting the FI's exposure to any single sector or single borrower to a certain percentage of the bank's capital irrespective of the credit standing of the borrower.

2. Liquidity Risk

Liquidity risk arises when liability holders, such as depositors, demand immediate cash for the financial claims (deposits) they hold with a FI or when holders of off-balance-sheet loan commitments (or credit lines) suddenly exercise their right to borrow (draw down their loan commitments). When depositors demand cash immediately, the FI must either borrow additional funds or sell assets to meet the demand for the withdrawal of funds. The most liquid asset of all is cash, which FIs can use directly to meet liability holders' demands to withdraw funds. Although FIs limit their cash asset holdings because cash does not earn interest, low cash holdings are generally not a problem.

Day-to-day withdrawals by liability holders are generally predictable, and banks can normally borrow additional funds from their respective central banks or from other banks through the interbank market to meet any sudden shortfalls of cash in the money and financial markets during normal line of activities. Furthermore, because most governments guarantee small depositors (less than $100,000 in the US and $10,000 in Lebanon, etc.), there is no need for small depositors to withdraw funds in a crisis.

In addition to an unusual or unexpected need for cash, a lack of confidence by depositors may lead to larger withdrawals than usual. When an FI faces abnormally large cash demands (e.g. Lebanese Canadian Bank in 2011), the cost of purchased or borrowed funds rises and the supply of such funds becomes restricted. As a consequence, The FI may have to sell some of its less liquid assets to meet the withdrawal demands of liability holders. This results in a more serious liquidity risk, especially as some assets generate lower prices when the sale is immediate than when an FI has more time to negotiate the sale of an asset. As a result, the liquidation of some assets at low or "fire-sale" prices (the price the FI receives if the assets must be liquidated immediately at less than their fair market value) could threaten the profitability and solvency of a financial institution.

Serious liquidity problems may eventually result in a "run" on the bank in which all liability claimholders seek to withdraw their funds simultaneously. This turns the FI's liquidity problem into a solvency problem and can cause it to fail.

Capital is not the best mitigate for liquidity risk, which is better managed by having an adequate buffer of high quality liquid assets and closely monitored liquidity limits. The quantification of liquidity risk is given by the Liquidity Coverage Ratio (LCR), defined as stock of high quality liquid asset divided by the expected net cash outflows (cash outflows less cash inflows) over the next 30 days. LCR is calculated on a quarterly basis and should always be greater than 100%. The stocks of high quality liquid asset include: government securities, excess current account balances with other banks and liquid corporate bonds of investment grade (BBB and above).

As for the liquidity concentration risk, the largest 20 depositors should not account for more than 5%-10% of total deposits. Furthermore, the FI should have a stable funding ratio designed to insure that long-term assets are funded with at least a minimum amount of stable resources over a one-year horizon. These sources include the bank's capital and liabilities with maturities of one year or more.

3. Interest Rate Risk

As part of their asset transformation function (collecting short term deposit to fund longer term loans and bonds), banks potentially expose themselves to interest rate risks. If the bank's assets are longer than its liabilities, it faces refinancing risk, defined as the risk that re-borrowing funds will rise above the returns being earned on asset investment. If the bank's assets are shorter than its liabilities, it faces reinvestment risk, which is the risk that the returns on funds to be reinvested will fall below the cost of funds.

All banks face price risk, or market value risk, when interest rates changes, because they are required to "mark to market" their trading portfolio. The economic or fair market value of an asset or liability is conceptually equal to the present value of the current and future cash flows on that asset or liability. Therefore, rising interest rates increase the discount rate on future asset (liability) cash flows and reduce the market price or present value of that asset or liability. Conversely, falling interest rates increase the present value of the cash flows from assets and liabilities. Moreover, mismatching maturities by holding longer-term assets than liabilities means that when interest rates rise, the economic or present value of the bank's assets will fall by a larger amount than do its liabilities. This exposes the bank to the risk of economic loss and potentially to the risk of insolvency.

Banks can hedge or protect themselves against interest rate risk by matching the maturity of their assets and liabilities. However, this approach is inconsistent with their asset transformation function and it may reduce their profitability. However, there are several methods to hedge interest rate risk using options, futures, and swaps.

4. Market Risk

This is the risk incurred in trading assets and liabilities due to changes in interest rates, exchange rates and other asset prices. The trading portfolios of financial institutions are differentiated from their investment portfolios on the basis of time horizon and liquidity. The trading portfolio contains assets, liabilities and derivative contracts that are highly liquid and are held for period of less than one year. Investment portfolios are relatively illiquid and are usually held for longer periods of time usually till maturity. The decline in traditional banking activities of Arab commercial banks have been offset by increases in their trading activities. Accordingly, fluctuations in income from trading portfolios (when these are marked to market) are having a bigger impact on the income statement of FIs in the region.

Trading or market risk is the risk that when a FI takes an open or unhedged long (buy) or short (sell) position in bonds, equities, commodities, and derivatives, prices may change in a direction opposite to that expected. As a result, as the volatility of asset prices increases, the market risks faced by FIs that adopt open trading positions increase. This requires the management of Arab financial institutions to establish controls for limits on positions taken by traders as well as to develop models to measure the market risk exposure of the bank on a day-to-day basis, the so called daily value at risk (VaR).

5. Off-Balance Sheet Risk

This is the risk incurred by banks as the result of activities related to contingent assets and liabilities (letters of credit, letters of guarantees, loan commitments, derivatives, etc.). An off-balance-sheet activity, by definition, does not appear on the bank's currant balance sheet. Instead, off-balance-sheet activities affect the future shape of the balance sheet because they involve the creation of contingent assets and liabilities that give rise to their potential placement in the future on the balance sheet.

The ability to earn fee income while not loading up or expanding the balance sheet has become an important motivation for banks in the region to pursue off-balance-sheet business. Unfortunately, this activity is not risk free. Suppose an importer defaults on a letter of credit issued for him by a bank, then the contingent liability or guaranty the bank has issued becomes an actual or real liability that appears on its balance sheet. That is, the bank has to use its own equity to compensate the exporter in whose name the letter of credit was issued. Indeed, significant losses in off-balance-sheet activities can cause a bank to fail, just as major losses due to balance sheet default and interest rates risks can do.

Letters of credit are just one example of off-balance-sheet activities. Others include loan commitments by banks and positions in forwards, futures, swaps, and other derivative securities held by almost all large FIs in the region. Although some of these activities are structured to reduce an FI's exposure to credit, interest rate, or other risks, mismanagement or speculative use of these instruments can result in major losses to FIs.

6. Foreign Exchange Risk

This is the risk that changes in currencies' exchange rates can adversely affect the value of a bank's assets and liabilities denominated in foreign currencies. Most FIs in the MENA region have an active US$ book both on the assets and liability sides of their balance sheet. Foreign exchange risks can occur either directly as the result of trading in foreign currencies, making loans in foreign currency especially US$, or buying foreign currency denominated securities, or having foreign currency deposits. Also indirectly by having a net long investment position or a net short investment position in a foreign currency.

A bank is fully hedged only when we assume that it holds an equal amount of foreign currency denominated assets and foreign currency denominated liabilities that have the same maturity. If the maturities are not matched, the bank could then be exposed to foreign interest rate risk. Consequently, an FI that matches both the size and maturities of its exposures in assets and liabilities of a given currency is hedged or immunized against foreign currency and foreign interest rate risk. To the extent that FIs mismatch their portfolio and maturity exposures in different currency assets and liabilities, they face both foreign currency and foreign interest rate risks (exposure of Lebanese, Jordanian and Gulf banks whose domestic currencies are pegged to the dollar when conducting banking operations through their branches in Syria, Egypt and Iraq). Because foreign exchange rate and interest rate changes are not correlated across countries, an FI can diversify away only a part, of its foreign currency risk.

7. Country or Sovereign Risk

Holding assets in foreign country through branches and/or subsidiaries can expose the bank to an additional type of foreign investment risk called country or sovereign risk. It is a different type of risk from credit risk that is faced by an FI that purchases domestic assets such as the bonds and the loans of domestic corporations. For example when a domestic corporation is unable or unwilling to repay a loan, the bank usually has recourse to the domestic bankruptcy court and eventually may recoup at least a portion of its original investment when the assets of the defaulted firm are liquidated or restructured. By comparison, a foreign corporation may be unable to repay the principal or interest on a loan even it would like to do so. Most commonly, the government of the country in which the corporation is headquartered may prohibit or limit debt repayments due to foreign currency shortages and adverse political events. Some Arab Countries who have experienced foreign currency shortages have invariably placed limits on capital outflows (e.g. Egypt, Syria).

Thus, sovereign risk is a broader measure of the risk faced by FIs that operate abroad. Measuring such exposure or risk includes an analysis of macroeconomic issues such as external and internal debt, foreign reserves, trade policy, the fiscal stance (deficit or surplus) of the government, as well as, the government's intervention in the economy, its monetary policy, capital flows, foreign investment, inflation and structure of its financial system. Even specific risks such as civil wars, revolutions, sudden market collapse should be taken in consideration. Credit rating by the major rating institutions (S&P, Moody's and Fitch) is the most indicative indicator of the country's sovereign risk.

8. Technology Risk

The major objectives of technological investment are to lower operating cost, increase profits and capture new markets. Technology risk occurs when technological investments do not produce the anticipated cost savings in the form of either economies of scale or economies of scope. Diseconomies of scale, for example, arise because of excess capacity, redundant technology, and/or organizational and bureaucratic inefficiencies (red tape) that become worse as the FI grows in size. Diseconomies of scope arise when an FI fails to generate perceived synergies or cost savings through major new technology investments. Technological risk can result in major losses to the FI's competitive efficiency and ultimately result in its long-term failure. Similarly, gains from technological investments can produce performance superior to an FI's rivals as well as allow it to develop new and innovative products enhancing its long-term survival chances.

9. Operational Risk

Operational and reputational risks are closely related. It is the risk of loss resulting from inadequate or failed internal processes, (control and audit), people and systems. Employee fraud, misrepresentations, and account errors comprise a type of operational risk that often negatively affect the reputation of a financial institution. A failed merger with another institution, as well as, the loss of computer back up that has names of customers or theft of credit cards constitute part of a broader definition of operational risk.

Mitigation and control measures of operational risk include buying insurance (fire/theft, etc.), putting in place business continuity plan with staff preparedness and disaster recovery site that has yearly maintenance and presence of highly trained and experienced staff. Capital allocation for operational risk is based on a scenario analysis that takes historical and expected loss events into consideration.

10. Insolvency Risk

Insolvency risk is the risk a financial institution may not have enough capital to offset a sudden decline in the value of its assets relative to its liabilities. It is usually the outcome of one or more of the risks described above. Technically, insolvency occurs when the equity of the FI is driven to zero as a result of losses.

Both regulators and managers focus on capital adequacy as a measure of an FI's ability to remain solvent in the face of a multitude of risk exposures. The more equity capital to total assets an FI has, the lower its leverage. The capital to assets or leverage ratio is defined as core capital (tier I) divided by assets, where core capital is common shareholders equity plus perpetual preferred stocks. If an FI's capital adequacy is 5% or higher it is generally, considered to be well capitalized. At 4% or more, it is adequately capitalized and less than 4% it is undercapitalized.

By taking total assets in the denominator the capital adequacy ratio does not account for the different credit, interest rate, market or operational risks of the assets, nor do we include off-balance-sheet activities. Another definition of capital adequacy was later introduced, called total risk based capital ratio defined as:

Total Risk-Based Capital Ratio=$\dfrac{\text{Tier1Capital+Tier2Capital}}{\text{Risk Adjusted Assets}}$

Where Tier 2 capital is a broad array of secondary capital resources, which, include general loan loss reserves up to 1.25% of risk adjusted assets and convertible debt instruments.

The risk-adjusted assets (both on balance sheet and off-balance-sheet) are derived by giving weights to different type of assets depending on their credit worthiness. For example, loans of banks to their own government denominated in the local currency irrespective of the country's rating are given zero weight. Loans to highly rated companies (AAA to A-) are given 20% weight, loans to companies rated A+ to A- (50% weight), loans to companies rated BBB+ to BB- (100% weight) and loans to companies rated below BB- (150% weight). To be adequately capitalized the total risk-based capital ratio must exceed 8.

Assume bank Audi lends $3 million to a corporate customer rated A- i.e. it has a credit risk weight of 50%. This can be converted into a risk-weighted asset of $1.5 million ($3 million x 50%). According to Basel II, the minimum capital required to support this loan is $120,000 ($1.5 million x 8%), where 8% is the risk based capital ratio.

If Bank Audi buys LL15 billion ($10 million) worth of CDs issued by the central bank of Lebanon, there will be a regulatory zero risk weight associated with this exposure and no capital allocation is needed to support such an exposure. This explains, at least partially, why commercial banks have a preference to increase exposure to their respective governments when loans extended and bonds bought are denominated in the local currency.

11.6 The Interaction of Various Risks

All the risks discussed above are interdependent. For example, when interest rates rise, corporations and consumers find maintaining promised payments on their debt more difficult. Thus, over some range of interest rate movements, credit and interest rates risks are positively correlated. Furthermore, the FI may have been counting on the funds from promised payments on its loans for liquidity management purposes. Thus, liquidity risk is also correlated with interest rate and credit risks. The inability of a customer to make promised payments also affects the FI's income and profits and, consequently, its equity or capital position. Thus, each risk and its interaction with other risks ultimately affects solvency risk. The interaction of the various risks also means that FI managers face making complicated trade-offs. In particular, as they take actions to manage one type of risk, FI managers must consider the possible impact of such actions on other risks.

Most of the risks we have considered in this chapter are termed known risks. They are risks such as market risks and credit risks that can be quantified using historical data. Two other types of risk are important to financial institutions: Unknown risks and unknowable risks.

Unknown risks are risks where the event that could cause a loss is known, but its probability of occurrence cannot easily be determined.

Operational risk includes many different types of unknown risks. What is the probability of a rogue trader loss? What is the probability of a loss from a major lawsuit? What is the probability that an uprising will take place in another Arab country? These probabilities cannot usually be estimated using historical data.

Some use the term "risk" to refer to known risks and the term "uncertainty" to refer to unknown risks. Unknowable risks are risks where even the event that could cause a loss is not known. Unknowable risks are in many ways the most insidious because they come as a complete surprise and often lead to dramatic losses. An unknowable risk is sometimes referred to as a black swan. (Black swans were not considered possible until they were discovered in Australia). Once it has occurred, a black swan event is often considered to be obvious. Did the producers of multi-volume encyclopedias in 1970 consider the possibility that online technological developments would render their product worthless? Probably not, but ex-post it seems a fairly obvious risk.

How can companies manage unknown and unknowable risks? A key tool is flexibility. Companies should avoid excessive leverage and try to insure that, as far as possible, their costs are variable rather than fixed. Diversification across products and markets also increases flexibility and reduces risks. Adequate capitalization of the financial institution remains the best protection against all types of risks. Based on a regression analysis of bank failure across various countries, capital adequacy and asset quality generally prove to be good predictive risk drivers of bank insolvency.

Chapter 12

The Path Ahead for MENA Finance

12.1 Introduction: The Need for Greater Financial Inclusion

The path ahead for MENA finance is now broadly clear. The relative weight of commercial banks in the financial system will diminish gradually, with a wider range of financial services to be provided by deeper and increasingly more sophisticated debt and equity capital markets, in line with worldwide trends.

From a development perspective, greater financial inclusion is positively correlated with GDP growth, and financial deepening has been proven to reduce inequality. Studies demonstrate for example, that access to microcredit increases by 50% the chances of hiring employees outside the household. Financial inclusion also brings down the cost of delivering public services. These services are significantly more efficient when delivered through the financial system (e.g. using plastic cards and electronic transfers for social benefits can cut costs for the government by over 80%) as opposed to through more paper-based mechanisms.

Although financial inclusion is not the solution to poverty, it remains an important milestone toward more inclusive social and economic systems. This would hold especially true in the Arab World, where 90% of the SMEs are informal, and where an estimated number of 8 million jobs need to be created every year for the coming decade.

Banks worldwide, required to hold more capital, are being pushed out of riskier areas of activities, especially long term lending and trading of bonds and other financial instruments. At the same time, asset management has been growing much faster outside the banking sector than within it, and all sorts of new payment technologies are springing up and new forms of finance are surfacing such as peer to peer (P2P) lending.

Private equity firms are branching out into private debt, lending directly to large companies. The European banks that were dominant in project finance credit in the MENA region are retrenching, leaving it to the bond market to fill the gap.

There is likely to be more alliances between banks and other financial institutions when providing long-term credit. Banks would respond to the financing requirements of their clients by doing the initial credit assessment and underwriting. They are likely to keep a slice of the loan on their books and syndicate the rest among insurance companies, pension funds and asset managers. The banks would free up part of their capital, the insurance and pension funds would get exposure to assets that they would not have been able to assess otherwise and borrowers will get funded.

Despite current limitations, the next ten years will record a surge of investment banking activities in the region. We are likely to see family businesses facing succession issues, others becoming fragmented, and divisions spun off and sold. Many private companies need to restructure or go public. Raising debt and equity and finding companies for acquisition will help support investment banking activities in the region. Privatization of few remaining government owned sectors in utilities, oil & gas and airlines would drive demand for advisory services.

Besides equity capital market activities, debt capital markets and M&A will also be needed in the next 10 years. As GCC public budgets become strained, governments will be increasingly relying on debt securities (bonds and Sukuk) to fund budget deficits and large-scale infrastructure projects. Also, businesses are maturing, and many of them would need long-term sources of funding, drawing on the bond market to support their expansion.

Islamic banking does cater to a very fast growing segment of the market. The demand for sharia compliant instruments has been growing regionally and internationally, and no financial Institution in the region can afford to ignore it, or avoid building capabilities to serve this segment. However, we are still in the trial and error phase, and we will continue to witness fast changes in regulations to deal with the arising risk, and the emergence of new products and structures.

It is unfortunate that well over half of the region's fresh graduates prefer the "security" of government jobs over any type of "riskier" private sector employment. This "brain drain" means less innovation, and fewer startups are being established and less exciting new jobs being created. The region needs a cultural shift whereby a higher proportion of graduates would follow their creative DNA and chose the more demanding path in life, that of innovation.

12.2 Equity Capital Markets and the Region's Stock Exchanges

Opening up the region's stock markets to international investors is a necessary but not a sufficient condition to attract institutional money needed to provide depth and professionalism to these markets. What global institutions look for more than anything else when exploring the world's capital markets is adherence to high standards of disclosure, regulation and governance, and presence of trustworthy counterparties to deal with. Without a cultural shift towards more transparency, enhancement of investor relations and corporate governance, and the availability of custody, clearance and equity research, up to international best practice, not much institutional money will be forthcoming to the region.

There is also a need to provide more tools for risk management such as lending of securities to short sell the markets, as well as, options and futures. MENA stock markets are inherently more volatile than their peers in other emerging markets. Managing this risk is a key underpinning for the entry of institutional investors.

To boost market liquidity and create a broader regional asset classes for investors, more consolidation of regional exchanges needs to take place, a trend that has been well adhered to internationally. The UAE continues to operate three exchanges two in Dubai and one in Abu Dhabi, while the other Arab countries operate their own single country exchange. Cross listing of companies and allowing brokers in one market to trade on the bourses of other countries through a local clearing member will help boost liquidity in these exchanges. An integration of the MENA exchanges would primarily entail aligning the policies and regulations under which the region's bourses operate. Each bourse would remain independent and continue to be regulated by local authorities, but rules and regulations would be standardized across all bourses. Such an initiative would presumably represent an interim step towards an ultimate region-wide consolidation.

To facilitate the process of mergers and acquisitions among exchanges more of them need to be converted into publically listed companies. To date only two Arab exchanges Dubai Financial Market (with 20% of its shares listed and traded on Dubai Exchange) and the Palestine Stock Exchange-which became a public shareholding company in 2010.

A private sector initiative that aims at establishing a Pan Arab Alternative Trading System (ATS) or what is known under European legislation, as Multilateral Trading Facility (MTF) should be considered. The aim is to have a platform that matches buyers and sellers to execute across border transactions. Such a platform would eventually lead to a Pan Arab exchange. The ATS will concentrate initially on Arab blue chip/large cap equities, as well as, ETFs and stock market indices. The platform will provide a clearing service and connectivity to settlement in each local jurisdiction.

There are many closed companies in the region, mainly family owned or private partnerships that could be groomed to become public shareholding companies but no one is showing them the way. The region's stock exchanges are called upon to establish a "second market" where closed companies would be listed and traded, similar to the initiative taken recently by the UAE. The second market would serve as incubator for closed companies, drawing on the consulting services of auditors and investment bankers in this respect. Many of the companies that would be carefully chosen to be listed on the second market may require restructuring and coaching for few years to help them make the transition from private to public. The process will give a much-needed push to the fledgling IPO markets of the region.

Stock markets should also start courting SMEs with a view to building new listings on the third tier segments of the exchanges similar to the trend observed internationally. Bank lending to SMEs in the region has been limited despite the subsidized funding made available by governments to banks to help support these enterprises. However, it is not cheap funding that banks lack, but the capital allocation needed to back the risky loans to SMEs. Luring these enterprises to issue shares on the region's stock markets will provide a new funding source to the SMEs.

UAE and Qatar were upgraded to Emerging market status in May 2014, which together with Egypt are the only three Arab countries in the MSCI emerging market Index. Most of the remaining Arab stock markets are in the MSCI frontiers market index, which includes 26 countries, and an estimated $24 billion of international funds tracking the index. Kuwait accounts for 28.1% of MSCI frontier index with 13 listed companies included, Oman accounts for 3.5% with 8 companies, Lebanon accounts for 2.6% with 5 companies, Jordan accounts for 0.9% with 4 companies, Tunisia accounts for 0.8% with 3 companies, and Bahrain accounts for 0.7% with 2 companies. Saudi Arabia falls under the category of MSCI stand alone country index.

Regulators in the region should do all what is needed in order to upgrade their respective stock markets from the "Frontier" to the "Emerging" market status and to become part of the MSCI Emerging Market Index. Regulations need to allow for the creation of market makers i.e. specialized institutions who would help build liquidity by guaranteeing bid/ask prices at all times. Stock lending and short selling is another requirement of MSCI, and rules restricting foreign ownership need to be relaxed.

Another requirement for the inclusion in the MSCI EM index is the introduction of a delivery versus payment (DvP) system for settlement of traded securities. Securities should be delivered to the buyer and cash received by the seller on the same day. DvP is a well-recognized procedure in the industry. Under the previous dual account system, the payment is made to the bank first, which then pays for the security. The risk of failure of the broker to deliver the shares bought and/or if there would be a forced sale of shares without the owner's consent remains in place. The DvP system relieves investors from taking an exposure risk to the brokers, besides it insures a seamless functioning of the payment and delivery procedure.

12.3 Developing Debt Capital Markets: Bonds and Sukuk

The region's debt capital markets could become a viable source to finance infrastructure projects. So far most projects in the region has been funded through bank debt and loans from export credit agencies. However, the new Basel III regulations that require banks to allocate more of their capital to long-term loans make lending for projects less profitable.

It is estimated that expenditures on infrastructure in the region could reach $2 trillion over the next 20 years. Project bonds provide a viable alternative to traditional bank financing. Furthermore, because Sukuk are based on real assets, they are naturally well suited to be used in project finance. Several Sukuk structures have been issued to finance projects in Malaysia and Saudi Arabia. For example, the SR 3.75 billion ($1 billion) Sukuk issued by SATORP in November 2011 to finance part of a new joint venture refinery owned by Aramco (62.5%) and Total (37.5%), is notable for its long-term tenure of 14 years and the fact that it is denominated in Saudi Riyals.

The region should also develop a market for high yield bonds, where regional companies below investment grade turn for finance. Moving down the credit curve is part of the natural development of the bond market. So far only few high yield bonds have been issued in the region. Dar Al Arkan, a listed Saudi real-estate development company, rated Ba3 by Moody's, issued $450 million Sukuk with 11% coupon. However, a high yield bond market will not take off unless the region addresses the illiquid nature of the secondary markets in these bonds.

A healthy secondary market in fixed income securities is important to mitigate liquidity concerns. Holding bonds and Sukuk to maturity will discourage institutional investors who seek efficient prices to help "mark to market" their investment portfolios. Having efficient market makers and allowing lending and borrowing of securities and the availability of trading information in a transparent way is key for improving liquidity and facilitating price discovery.

If sufficient supply of new issues of various maturities comes to the market regularly it will greatly boost secondary market liquidity. This should be complemented with efficient and safe settlement, clearing and custody services. Many institutional investors do not want to take the counterparty risk of local custodians and would prefer the internationally established institutions to provide settlement and custody services in the markets of the region.

The region needs to position itself as a global center for Sukuk. The absence of a substantial debt capital market across a large and wealthy part of the world covering the MENA region, Africa and most of Asia excluding Japan, explains at least partially the serious imbalance we have in world financial flows, i.e. from emerging into developed markets than the other way round.

12.4 Developing Supportive Financial Infrastructure

A frequently quoted problem for the development of an Arab Financial Center is the lack of large vicinity. London is locked into the EU with 490 million residents and a GDP of nearly $23 trillion. New York has a hinterland of 300 million residents in the US and a GDP of $17 trillion. The Arab countries have limited immediate vicinity, as the MENA region does not constitute a substantial launch pad for a major financial center. Expanding into the Indian Subcontinent, the ex-Soviet (CIS countries) and the rest of Africa, could position the region as a global center for Sukuk. This would help countries of these regions finance infrastructural projects and would provide a profitable outlet to a huge pool of Islamic funds in the Gulf.

The absence of a centralized, global regulator in Islamic finance has so far been a double-edged sword. On the positive side, it gave financial institutions certain freedom in structuring products and marketing them as sharia compliant, which helped the industry to grow and prosper. On the other hand, there is a risk of an inconsistent application of the principles of Islamic finance, which may result in greater confusion and ultimately the loss of faith in these principles. What is needed is a central regulator, providing proper and consistent legal and regulatory framework that brings clarity and reliability to this market, playing the same role as the Basel Committee does for conventional banks.

Arab exchanges currently act as centerpieces of state-driven financial sector development strategies. Accordingly, changing the ownership structure of exchanges from public to privately listed institutions need to be carefully considered in any future plans to develop financial centers and related infrastructure. Looking outside the region, empirical evidence suggests that private ownership of exchanges have contributed positively to the exchange performance and wider financial markets development.

The fact that all the MENA exchanges have their own proprietary systems (from trading platforms to settlement and clearing) makes it very difficult for companies to cross-list their shares. This stands in clear contrast to the highly interconnected and well-integrated European bourses, where the logistical back-end of moving shares from one market to another works very well. Absent an exchange consolidation or complete systems standardization, the ability of companies to cross-list their shares within the region will remain limited.

Arab banks are still not ready to cope with the increasing threat from a growing number of digital companies (crowdfunding, peer-to-peer lending, etc.) who are working to capture market share from traditional players. The retail banking business model has a number of significant challenges to overcome if they to survive the digital onslaught. Such a threat will shorten the lifespan of banks similar to what we have seen in other sectors like Telco (e.g. WhatsApp), media and travel (e.g. Uber and Airbnb).

There is a three-stage scenario that looks likely to play out. Firstly, banks will get displaced by new entrants offering a better customer experience and price, second, bank revenues will be diminished in a market of higher switching frequency where banking services are relegated to undifferentiated utilities, before finally their core competency of storing and transferring value is challenged by the arrival of a new technology that is likely to dis-inter mediate the banks completely.

Obstacles that banks face (legacy technology, rapidly changing consumer behavior and lack of digital expertise and knowledge) are too great for them to overcome from within. Banks in the region have to radically rethink their operating models and explore possibilities of establishing partnership with digital companies to rebuild their unsecured consumer lending and cope with the fundamental changes brought about by new technologies.